Helen Thayer
& Charlie

POLAR DREAM

HELEN THAYER

FOREWORD BY SIR EDMUND HILLARY

SIMON & SCHUSTER

NEW YORK • LONDON • TORONTO • SYDNEY • TOKYO • SINGAPORE

SIMON & SCHUSTER

Simon & Schuster Building

Rockefeller Center

1230 Avenue of the Americas

New York, New York 10020

Simon & Schuster and colophon are

registered trademarks of Simon & Schuster Inc.

Designed by Barbara M. Bachman

Manufactured in the

United States of America

10 9 8 7 6 5 4 3 2 1

Library of Congress

Cataloging-in-Publication Data

Thayer, Helen.

   Polar dream : the heroic saga of the first solo journey by
a woman and her dog to the Pole / Helen Thayer.

      p.   cm.

   1. Thayer, Helen—Journeys.   2. North Pole.
3. Women explorers.   I. Title.

G630.N48T47   1993

910′.91432—dc20   92-41445

                                                  CIP

ISBN 0-671-79386-1

Photos courtesy of author's collection.

TO MY HUSBAND, BILL,

AND MY PARENTS,

RAY AND

MARGARET NICHOLSON,

WHOSE LOVE AND

ENCOURAGEMENT

URGED ME ONWARD.

CONTENTS

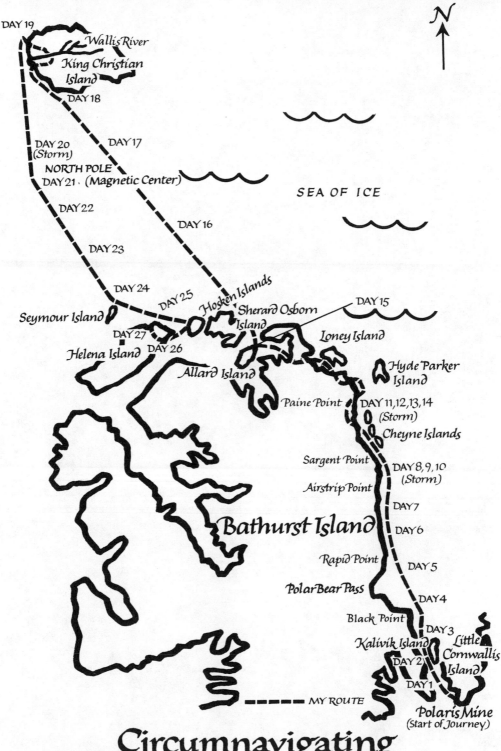

N

DAY 19
Wallis River
King Christian
Island
DAY 18

DAY 20
(Storm)
DAY 17

NORTH POLE
DAY 21 (Magnetic Center)

SEA OF ICE

DAY 22

DAY 16

DAY 23

DAY 24
DAY 25
Hocken Islands
Sherard Osborn
Island
DAY 15

Seymour Island
Loney Island

DAY 27
Helena Island
DAY 26
Allard Island
Hyde Parker
Island

Paine Point
DAY 11,12,13,14
(Storm)

Cheyne Islands

Sargent Point
DAY 8,9,10
(Storm)

Airstrip Point

Bathurst Island
DAY 7

DAY 6

Rapid Point
DAY 5

Polar Bear Pass
DAY 4

Black Point
DAY 3
Kalivik Island
Little
Cornwallis
Island
DAY 2

DAY 1

- - - - - MY ROUTE

Polaris Mine
(Start of Journey)

Circumnavigating
the Magnetic North Pole Area

FOREWORD

BY

SIR EDMUND HILLARY

≡ I first met Helen Thayer when she was attending a small high school near Auckland, in New Zealand. The headmaster, Dan Bryant, a renowned alpinist and a close friend of mine, energetically encouraged his students to meet the challenges of mountain climbing. No one responded more enthusiastically than Helen Thayer. She developed a deep love for the mountains, and went on to climb a multitude of great peaks all over the world.

But nothing Helen has done was more difficult and challenging than her solo journey in 1988 to the magnetic North Pole. She traveled alone, on foot or skis, pulling her supplies and equipment on a sled. Her only companion was a big black husky she had met only three days before she began her journey. She called the dog Charlie, and together they embarked on an expedition that lasted twenty-seven days and covered 364 miles. During that arduous journey, a unique bond between them was woven and strengthened. Charlie, a work dog that had never been treated like a pet or a partner, learned for the first time to bond with a human. He taught Helen the ways of Arctic survival and even saved her life from marauding polar bears. They began the journey as strangers and returned as inseparable friends.

But this is just one aspect of the enthralling story of a woman who at the age of fifty took an extraordinary journey that brought her to the edge of emotional and physical survival—an epic undertaking that few people of any age or sex could have achieved. Helen faced sub-zero temperatures, rough and cracking ice, fierce Arctic storms, frostbite, hunger, and menacing polar bears. But her discipline and unwavering motivation kept her going despite all obstacles, until she reached her goal and she and Charlie returned safely.

Helen recorded her experience in the journal she kept during her journey, carefully noting not only the physical challenges she continually faced, but also her own deep emotional reactions to the dangers and isolation of the Arctic regions. Her journal became the basis for this book—a remarkable odyssey by a truly remarkable woman.

INTRODUCTION

≡ The idea seemed rather far-fetched at first. Polar
expeditions are not new, of course. In recent years, they
have been undertaken with increasing frequency and
increasing sophistication: snowmobiles instead of
dogsleds, airplanes resupplying and supporting well-
equipped teams experienced in the dangers of polar exploration. But my idea *was* new: a solo journey to the
world's magnetic North Pole, a journey on foot and skis,
no dog teams or snowmobiles and no more equipment
than I could pull behind me on a sled. I would be the
first woman to make such a journey. And I was fifty
years old.

I was also an experienced mountain climber. I grew up on a large farm in New Zealand that I remember for its sprawling emerald-green pastures that stretched across rolling hills where sheep and cattle grazed. My parents, hard-working and disciplined, often went mountain climbing and one day when I was nine, they and some friends decided to climb Mount Egmont, a snow-capped 8,258-foot peak. To my delight, they invited me to go with them. "If you can carry your own pack," they said, "you can go."

After that climb, I couldn't resist the thought of becoming a real mountain climber like the people I admired. Besides my parents and their friends, my hero was Sir Edmund Hillary, a fellow New Zealander who, in 1953, became the first person to climb Mount Everest. When Hillary went to the South Pole in 1958, I dreamed that someday I, too, would go to one of the world's poles.

Over the years that followed, I guess I was secretly preparing for my polar expedition. I loved outdoor sports, especially winter sports. I competed in international track and field events, at times representing New Zealand, Guatemala, and the United States. After watching luge races on television in 1972 and envying the thrill of racing down thin ribbons of ice on a tiny sled with no brakes, I took up the sport and won the United States National Championship in 1975. But after representing the United States in luge competition in Europe, I realized something about myself. I didn't really enjoy competing against others. I found more pleasure competing against myself, setting goals and meeting the challenge of attaining them.

I returned to my first love, mountain climbing, and since then I've reached the summits of the highest mountains in New Zealand, North and South America, the Soviet Union, and one of the highest in China. It was while I stood in the thin air of the 23,405-foot summit of Peak Lenin in the Pamirs of the Soviet Union in 1986 that I decided the time had come to realize my polar dream, and I began to lay out a plan as I descended the mountain.

Ever since I was a young girl in New Zealand, I have been fascinated by the polar regions of the world, and as I learned more about them I experienced a growing curiosity about the magnetic North Pole, in particular. After all, over the years as I navigated my way through the valleys and over the ridges of mountain ranges, my compass needle always pointed to the magnetic North Pole. I, too, was drawn in that direction. I wondered what it would be like to go there, and as I descended Peak Lenin I decided this would be the pole I would attempt to reach.

Flying back to my home in Washington State, I was anxious to talk over my idea with Bill, my husband and best friend. Bill supported me in everything I did, and his mountain-climbing and expedition experience would give him a total understanding of the journey I contemplated. Indeed, he enjoyed a challenge himself and had a curiosity that always wanted to "see over the other side." My mother and father had also supported me through all sorts of sports and adventures. More than parents, they, too, had always been my close friends. I was eager to share my plans with them too.

Bill met me at the Seattle airport and within minutes I had told him of my new decision to travel to the magnetic North Pole. He was immediately enthusiastic. "A woman has never soloed any of the world's poles," he said with excitement. "It's a great idea." But how to turn that idea into reality? We began by looking at a budget and ways to pay for the expedition. After much pencil sharpening we arrived at a figure of ten thousand dollars. We could scrape that much together over the next two years, giving us time to read and research the Arctic, while gathering the necessary specialized equipment.

Next day I telephoned my parents in Whangarei, New Zealand. "Well, you've talked about the poles for a long time," Mother said. "I think the time is right and you should go, but what about the polar bears?" At the mention of polar bears Dad quickly came on the line. "What's this about polar bears? What are you planning now?" When I told him, he was apprehensive about the bears, but after I reassured him that if it appeared to be too dangerous I wouldn't go, he became excited about the journey and eagerly discussed logistics. Mother already had suggestions about clothing and food.

Some of my friends just shook their heads when I told them of my idea. "It's crazy, a woman can't survive out there alone," one friend told me. Another said, "You'll never come back alive. Forget it, go somewhere safer." Fortunately, others made more positive comments and even wrote letters of encouragement.

Although I knew my compass always pointed to the magnetic North Pole, I really didn't know much else about it. So I decided to talk to the scientists who study and track the pole each year. Canadian government scientists in Ottawa told me that when discussing the location of the pole, they refer only to an average position. The magnetic North Pole cannot be defined as a dot on the map. Instead, it is an elusive target in constant motion as it travels a daily, jagged, elliptical path in a clockwise direction over a wide area, sometimes moving more than a hundred miles in a single day.

The cause of this erratic movement is the sun. As the pole slowly drifts northwest, the sun constantly emits charged particles, which, as they encounter the earth's magnetic field, produce electrical currents in the upper atmosphere. These electric currents disturb the magnetic field, resulting in a shift in the pole's position. The distance and speed of the pole's movement depends on disturbances within the magnetic field, but the pole is constantly moving, sometimes slowly, sometimes rapidly.

Scientists who try to determine the average position of the pole must take into account all of its transient wanderings and can, at best, come up with only an average position. Even they sometimes differ from each other in their calculations by several miles. Therefore, the pole area covers a wide expanse. But because a compass points to the vicinity of the magnetic North Pole, it is used throughout the world as a vital navigational tool by sailors, aviators, and land travelers. Within the vicinity of the pole, however, a compass is completely useless, turning lazily and unpredictably in all directions due to the lack of horizontal magnetic pull.

In 1988, the year I planned to make my journey, the magnetic North Pole would be situated in the Northwest Territories of northern Canada, south of King Christian Island, a barren, lonely, windswept, ice-covered island that lies almost eight hundred miles north of the Arctic Circle. My plan, as it evolved, was to fly from Seattle, near my home in Washington State, to Resolute Bay, a tiny Inuit village of about 250 people on Cornwallis Island in the Northwest Territories. It was the traditional gathering place for past polar expeditions. I would pack my sled and take the short fifty-seven-mile flight northwest from Resolute Bay to Little Cornwallis Island. The people working at the Polaris lead and zinc mine on the island would be the last humans I would encounter after I started my journey. From there my route would take me about 350 miles, depending on detours around mounds of rough ice and other obstacles, through a maze of barren islands and across a vast expanse of sea ice, home to polar bears but a place where no humans have ever lived.

I knew this expedition would be a test of every outdoor skill I possessed. The possibility of minus-50-degree temperatures, hurricane-force winds, and sea ice that could split beneath me at any moment loomed large in my mind as I tried to think of every danger I might face. Of course the greatest danger would be the polar bears. The Inuit call them nanuk and tell tales of a stealthy, silent animal that sometimes hunts and kills humans for food. I had confidence in my outdoor abilities, which had been fine-tuned over many years. But I had yet to encounter a polar bear.

I had decided I would walk and ski to the pole pulling my own sled behind me, without resupply by aircraft or snowmobile. Traveling the entire distance, living with only the food and equipment I could pull in my sled, appealed to me as a demanding challenge and as a method that would have an environmentally low impact on my surroundings. Knowing the physical demands of traveling on foot, pulling a heavily loaded sled behind me, I embarked on a rigorous endurance program. In addition to climbing and skiing in the nearby Cascade Mountains, I ran ten miles a day through the forest, lifted weights in our basement gym, and kayaked on Storm Lake, where the blue herons looked on in wonder as I paddled up and down the lake for an hour at a time.

While gathering my equipment, I read all I could

about the Arctic and polar bears. Still, I knew that I would have to test the equipment "on location" at Resolute Bay before finally deciding what to take on the expedition. I telephoned Bezal Jesudason, an Arctic tourist outfitter who was born in India and graduated with an engineering degree from a German university. While working in Canada, he married Terry, a Canadian girl, and moved to Resolute Bay, where he set up an outfitting business. He invited me to fly to Resolute and stay at his inn. I flew there in November 1987. Winter had begun and the days were already only six hours long and the sea ice in the bay was freezing into a solid, white sheet.

As a defense against polar bears, I borrowed a rather ancient-looking shotgun from Bezal, who assured me that it was in good working order. "Anyway," he said, "the bears will be more afraid of you than you are of them. They haven't seen a woman out there alone before." I hoped he was right as I started out on a five-day journey to test my equipment. I just couldn't imagine a polar bear being scared of anything, let alone a woman who had so much to learn about the Arctic and who had only seen polar bears at the zoo. But polar bears or not, it was important for me to experience the aloneness and silence of the Arctic, depending only on myself. That challenge worried me just as much as polar bears.

The ice of Resolute Bay was rock-hard and slippery and I had to stretch ski-skins, long strips of synthetic material, along the underside of my skis to prevent them from skidding. They also prevented my skis from sliding backward when I pulled a heavily loaded sled, which had been strengthened to withstand the rough ice and low temperatures. I tried different types of clothing, tents, and stoves. I even practiced taking 35-

millimeter photos of myself, a necessity of a solo journey. After the tip of my nose became frostbitten when it touched the metal camera, I decided to add a good neoprene mask to my equipment list.

As for my choice of clothing, I narrowed it down to a windproof jacket with a hood, a nylon fleece under-jacket, another lighter-weight fleece jacket, and finally, two layers of synthetic "long johns" with high necks to keep the wind and blowing snow out. My gloves were large insulated mitts, with lighter mittens underneath and thin liner gloves next to my skin. A sturdy tent would be an essential on my journey and I chose a two-person, double-walled, three-poled structure, which, with no wind, I could erect in three minutes. However, after I tossed my large down sleeping bag and other gear into the tent, it was immediately reduced to a one-person model with no room to spare. My living quarters would be adequate, but not roomy. I chose an MSR stove; they are noisy but very reliable and burn white gas, which I could buy in Resolute.

After five days alone on the sea ice, I was somewhat more confident I could handle the solitude and silence of an Arctic journey. I skied back to land, looking forward to talking to people once more and hearing sounds other than the grinding and the groaning of the ice pack beneath my feet. I had seen no sign of polar bears, which was a relief, and I was satisfied with my choice of equipment. But I knew this had been merely a test run, not the real thing.

Back at the inn, I arranged with Bezal to rent a high-frequency radio for the duration of my expedition, so that I could call him and Terry each night while I was traveling to the pole. Their inn would become my base camp, as it had for earlier Arctic expeditions. I would be alone on the ice, but my location would always be known in case of an emergency.

I walked over to the airport to meet Ruddi Kellar, the base manager of Bradley Air Services, a charter operation of Twin Otters that flies to many parts of the Arctic. I talked over my expedition plans with Ruddi and he agreed to send a plane to pick me up at the end of my journey.

Before leaving Resolute, I talked to some of the local Inuit about my journey. At first they were aghast at the idea of a woman even thinking of such a trip, let alone traveling by myself on foot. I was urged by some to travel by snowmobile, while others thought the only way I could survive would be to take a dog team. But pulling my own sled behind me was a method I had used for many years climbing mountains with long glacier approaches, which had to be crossed before reaching the start of the actual climb. I stuck to my original plan.

Tony, an Inuit polar bear hunter, was particularly concerned about my safety without a dog team. Inuit dogs and polar bears are natural enemies, and a dog team would be my best protection against marauding bears. I listened carefully to his warnings and concerns. Then, hoping he could understand my logic, I replied, "If I'm going to make this journey, I want to use human power and depend on my own skills, rather than use a dog team." As for polar bears, I believed I could travel safely on foot as long as I took a firearm and flare gun for protection. I reasoned that the flare gun would be a good, nonlethal warning device, while the firearm would be a last resort. The Inuit, who hunt polar bears with high-powered rifles, favored a rifle over a shotgun. But I wanted a firearm only as a defensive weapon. I decided to make the final decision about what kind of gun to take after talking to people experienced in self-defense against large animals.

Soon it was time to say good-bye to my new friends in Resolute. While talking and listening to the Inuit, I developed the utmost respect for their survival skills and knowledge of the Arctic. I decided to take another two weeks of training at Resolute Bay with the Inuit immediately before beginning my expedition in March 1988. Those two weeks would give me an opportunity to learn more from the Inuit about polar bears and how I would have to deal with them.

Back home, as I continued to prepare for my journey, I was surprised to find how little had been written about the Arctic, and I realized my expedition would present a unique opportunity to collect geographical, historical, and scientific information, which could become a school educational program. The idea was received with enthusiasm by the teachers I spoke to. The Arctic was virtually unknown to schoolchildren. Because I would be traveling on foot to the pole, I could enter detailed descriptions of everything I saw into an extensive journal. I could describe the landscape and the places named after early Arctic explorers. I could describe the sea ice and the wildlife that lived and hunted on it. I could record details of weather and temperatures and describe what it was like to live in such an environment. After my return, the information I gathered, illustrated by my photographs, would go to schools to create a better understanding of a little-known place. While realizing my own dream, I also hoped to increase an awareness among schoolchildren of the delicate environment of the Arctic and the need to protect it.

The idea of my journey as the basis for an educational

project inspired a change in my plans. I decided that rather than travel to the pole area and immediately be flown back to base camp, I would travel throughout the area to better understand and photograph the islands surrounding the pole. When scientists in Ottawa learned of my expedition and my intention to travel extensively within the pole area, they asked me to collect snow samples and temperature data, which they would use in their continuing study of the Arctic environment.

Soon it was March 1988 and I was ready to leave for Resolute Bay. I loaded our small yellow 1976 Datsun pickup truck with a wooden box full of my equipment and drove for three hours, crossing the international border to Vancouver, to air freight my sled and skis to Resolute Bay. Two days after my freight left, it was time for me to leave. I had been so busy preparing for the adventure ahead of me that I hadn't given any thought to what my feelings would be when I had to say good-bye to Bill, my parents, and friends. I have never been very good at good-byes and really dreaded this one because I knew people would worry about me since I was traveling alone.

I called my parents in New Zealand, and as they wished me luck, I only just held back my tears. After all, I told myself, I'm not leaving forever. Bill, a commercial helicopter pilot who was flying at the time in Florida, managed to get a few days off to take me to the airport. We had decided earlier that because we were financing the expedition ourselves, he would continue working rather than accompany me to Resolute Bay.

I was truly looking forward to the expedition, but first of all I had to somehow get through saying good-bye. As Bill and I drove to the airport, I made a stern resolution not to cry, aware that I had unsuccessfully made this resolution often in the past. Every time my parents visited us in the United States and we, in turn, visited them in New Zealand, I went through the same tearful scene.

Bill was unusually quiet as we drove over the Canadian border to the Vancouver airport, so I said, "Let's make it easy on ourselves and make it a fast good-bye."

"Sounds good to me," he said.

We arrived at the airport, and after checking in at the ticket counter we hugged. "See you," I said, and turned to leave with as much composure as possible. I didn't dare look back. Then I heard a loud "I love you." "I love you too," I called back, and then hurried to board the plane as I fought back the tears. I was crying, of course.

1.

CHARLIE

Our plane landed on the icy runway in Resolute Bay amid a flurry of fine-grained snow whipped into the air by the jet engines. I stared out the window surprised at the darkness that embraced the tiny settlement. It was mid-March and Bezal had told me over the phone two weeks ago that I could expect nineteen to twenty hours of daylight by the end of March. I had hoped to begin my journey to the pole in long daylight hours so that I could see the polar bears more easily. I climbed down from the plane to greet Bezal, and even before the usual salutations I asked with anxiety, "What happened to the daylight?" "Be patient, it'll come," he replied. I hope so, I thought to myself. It could be a bit tricky living with polar bears in this darkness.

We loaded my two seventy-pound red duffel bags onto his pickup truck, stuffed two more smaller bags and my camera gear inside the barely warm cab, and began the five- or six-mile drive from the airport to the village. Resolute is really two settlements; the one surrounding the airport is known as the Base and consists mainly of government buildings, while the village is an Inuit settlement of small wooden houses clustered together along short, narrow streets that wander aimlessly without any real direction.

Bezal and Terry's High Arctic Inn is at the edge of the village, and we arrived in time for Terry's plentiful dinner. We ate family style, with a half dozen other guests, who were dumbfounded when they learned I was going to walk to the magnetic North Pole.

After dinner I began moving all my gear into the inn's garage where my sled and skis already sat in a corner. A few of the guests wandered over, obviously to check to see if they had understood me correctly. Two men from Germany who had come to hunt seals were appalled that a woman would actually try to walk to the pole. They looked at the .338 magnum Winchester rifle and the flare gun I intended to use for protection against polar bears and laughed. "This has far too much kick for a woman your size, you need something smaller."

I drew myself up to my full five feet three inches and told them, with as much conviction as possible, that the gun had been recommended to me by someone who hunted big game in Africa, and that I had joined our local gun club so that I could practice. Actually, I wasn't really sure that I had the right firearm. I had never before been given so many conflicting pieces of advice in my life.

As I packed a few things in the bottom of my sled, a visiting dentist, who wanted "a quiet vacation far from civilization," lifted one end of the sled and declared, "This is far too long and heavy for you to pull all that way. You won't last three days." He was joined by an Austrian tourist who wanted "to see Arctic wildlife." With an air of authority he told me, "Two things will get you. One, the bears, and two, the cold. The first bear will scare you to death."

I started to reply, but decided to let it go. I had heard all the negative opinions I could handle for one day and anyway it was bedtime.

At five the next morning, while everyone was still asleep, I ate a quick breakfast of cold cereal and went out to the garage to pack my sled, this time alone. I had chosen the food for my journey with great care. Supplies of rice, milk powder, chocolate powder, oatmeal, granola, crackers, peanut butter cups, walnuts, and cashew nuts packed in plastic bags went into large stuff sacks. The high-carbohydrate powder I would use for drinking was already packaged and slipped into the bottom of each sack, one for each week. I was taking enough food for forty days, but expected the journey to last no more than thirty. I bought white gas from Bezal for my stove, plus two extra gallons for safety. All my cooking and drinking water would have to be melted. I would rather take too much fuel than risk dehydration.

Bezal and Terry had agreed to listen for my radio call each night at eight during my journey, when I would take out my six-pound, battery-powered, high-frequency, receiver-transmitter radio and call base camp, giving my exact location after each day's travel. If they didn't hear from me for four days, Bezal would launch a search based on my last known position. I had promised Bill, my parents, and friends at home that I would contact base camp by radio each night. It would be my only safety net during the expedition.

By midmorning everything was sorted and packed and people began drifting by, among them some of the Inuit who had spoken with me last November. They had obviously given my journey more thought and still weren't convinced I should go. One tall fellow whose name I could never pronounce said, "You're making a mistake, you shouldn't go without a dog team or snow-mobile."

"I'll be OK if I learn all I can about bears and how to react around them," I replied. "I've got time before I leave. Will you teach me?"

His quick and eager reply was, "Meet me here at the garage at two this afternoon and we'll go down to the ice. Bring your rifle, ammunition, and flare gun."

At two o'clock he was there waiting with four friends, his snowmobile, and a kamotik, an Inuit wooden sled. I wasn't going to be short of instructors. Two on the snowmobile and the rest of us bumping along behind on the kamotik soon covered the quarter mile down to the sea ice. My lesson began with gruesome stories about what damage a polar bear can do to a human body. I suspected that it was part of a plan to persuade me to abandon my travel plans. I held up my hand and said, "I already know that a bear is capable of killing me. What I need to learn is how to avoid being killed." With that, my instructors changed course and enthusiastically taught me how to react when faced by a bear, what signs to look for when watching for bears, and how bears hunt.

Out on the bay we found bear tracks and I learned to distinguish between new and old tracks and how to tell whether the bear was male or female. I was told that a bear hunts silently. "You'll never hear a bear come up behind you; you'll know he's come for you when he pounces, then it's too late." I practiced firing at a two-foot-high chunk of ice from all positions at minus 33 degrees Fahrenheit, using gloves to protect my fingers from freezing to the metal parts of the rifle. At last my instructors were satisfied that I was proficient with the rifle and I had a good understanding of polar bears. The Inuit survival skills have been passed down through countless generations; they survive almost by instinct, whereas I had to learn things they take for granted. My respect for the Inuit and polar bears continued to grow.

The next day was stormy so I took my tent down to the sea ice to practice erecting it in the wind. I skied out into the bay to feel the cold wind in my face, watching for bears and getting the feel of the ice pack beneath my skis. I spent several more days training out on the ice pack, sometimes alone and sometimes with the Inuit, who were always checking to find out if I was still learning and remembering all that they had told me.

It was while I was packing my sled for yet another training run that Tony came by. I had met him the past November and hoped to talk to him before I left for the pole, but he had been out on the sea ice hunting polar bears. He owned one of the better dog teams in Resolute and in November had been very vocal about the negative aspects of my travel plans. As soon as he returned from hunting and heard that I was preparing to leave on the expedition, he came over and tried to persuade me not to go. "There is still a lot of darkness," he said with a worried frown. "You won't see the bears. They'll come to your tent while you sleep. No matter what sort of rifle you have, you won't hear them while you sleep. If you must go, take a dog team. You'll be faster. Three or four dogs will be enough, I can teach you."

I told Tony I still didn't want a dog team but I had been wondering about taking just one dog to walk alongside me to warn of approaching bears during the day and be on guard at night.

With a look of great relief, Tony grinned and said, "I've got a dog you can take. He's trained to warn the village of approaching polar bears and he knows how to take care of himself."

When I agreed to at least take a look at the dog, Tony left and returned with a big, black, docile husky. I fell in love with him at first sight. I had no idea what he thought of me. I suppose he didn't care who owned him as long as he was fed and taken care of. He didn't look particularly brave or ferocious and I wondered just what kind of experience he might have had with polar bears. I wondered, too, how he would hold up to the rigors of my journey. He knew even less than I did about what we might expect along the way. But there was something about him I thought I could trust and I decided to take him with me. I bought him from Tony and when I took his chain he came to me willingly enough. Perhaps he thought he could trust me too.

This dog, like most Inuit dogs, had no name. I decided to call him Charlie, and the first thing I had to do was find a sheltered place for him to sleep. I couldn't take him inside the inn with me. I knew better than to ask. Inuit dogs are never invited indoors. But now that Charlie was mine, I didn't want him left uncared for out on the ice. After hunting around I found a rather sad-looking boat that was used when the ice thawed during the short summer. The boat was stuck fast in the solid ice, leaning at a precarious angle, its torn canvas awning frozen in a fly-away position. I tied Charlie to the stern and he lost no time jumping inside. I fed him, then watched as he finished his dinner, curled up inside the boat, and fell fast asleep.

The next morning I was up at first light to go back to the boat and greet my new friend. Inuit dogs lead a harsh life. They're not treated as pets, but rather as animals that have to learn how to survive. A piece of frozen seal meat is tossed to them two or three times a week and they chew ice while living tied to a four-foot chain. They're given no shelter, even during bitter midwinter Arctic storms. I had more humane ideas about how to treat Charlie, but the local Inuit weren't used to seeing a dog fussed over and some expressed the opinion that I would ruin him. Nevertheless I continued with my fussing in the hope that Charlie would learn to love and trust me. After all, my life might depend on his loyalty.

With only three days left before I began my journey, I had to hurry and gather equipment for Charlie. A visiting dogsledder gave him a blue plastic child's sled and a shiny red harness. Charlie's thick black coat looked magnificent with his new harness in place and the little sled was perfect for carrying his food. An Austrian dog-sledding team that had turned back from a geographic North Pole expedition because of severe frostbite to the leader's hands and feet gave Charlie all the dog food he would need for the journey. I loaded eighty-five pounds of dry dog food in sacks onto his sled, enough for two pounds a day plus extra in case of an emergency. Terry gave me an old aluminum two-quart saucepan with no handle that made a perfect feeding dish.

I took Charlie out onto the sea ice to begin our training together. He didn't like the cold, hard ice and decided to solve that problem by standing squarely on both of my skis. I explained to him that as long as he had me anchored to the spot, we weren't able to go anywhere. He wasn't interested in going anywhere, but after a few minutes I convinced him that I would ski on the skis and he would walk on the ice at my side. He had never seen skis before so it must have been with some degree of amazement that he watched me move about on those very long "feet."

The plan was for Charlie to pull his sled loaded with 85 pounds of his food, while I pulled my seven-foot-long blue fiberglass sled loaded with 160 pounds of food, fuel, clothing, tent, and equipment. Tony told me to keep Charlie tethered at my side while I traveled so that he would always be with me, instead of racing around after polar bears and possibly getting lost. I bought a new, blue nylon collar and sturdy dog chain with a quick-release clip. I attached Charlie's chain to a loop on my sled harness at my waist, making it impossible for him to go anywhere without me. He soon grew used to walking at my right side, keeping up with me. Within three days, Charlie and I had become a team. He was even learning his name.

On March 29, Charlie and I finished our training at Resolute Bay and were flown in a DC3 about fifty-seven miles northwest to the Polaris lead and zinc mine. This Canadian-owned operation—the northernmost metal mine in the Western world—is located on Little Cornwallis Island and was the logical place to begin my journey. All our gear and both sleds had been loaded on board the DC3 along with a cargo of potatoes and other food bound for the mine. Charlie and I were the only passengers. I was squeezed into a tiny seat up front behind the pilot's cabin and I kept a tight grip on Charlie's collar as we took off on the ice-covered runway, not knowing how he would react to flying. His first reaction was surprise. All ninety-three pounds of him immediately climbed onto my lap.

The copilot came back to check on us. "How are you doing back here?" he asked. Spitting black fur out of my mouth and trying to see the pilot around Charlie without much success, I answered with a muffled, "Just fine."

When he left I levered Charlie onto the window half of my seat, and I sat wedged between him and a large sack of potatoes. It wasn't a very romantic way to begin my journey but it would have to do. Meanwhile, Charlie settled in nicely, greatly reducing my portion of the seat as he relaxed. Finally I gave up and sat half on the seat and half on the potatoes.

For thirty minutes we flew over a barren, frozen landscape. As I looked past Charlie's head at the ice-covered terrain below, it seemed very uninviting, but I reasoned that everything would be all right once we were on the ground and out of this cramped, unheated, potato-filled plane.

We landed at Polaris on yet another frozen, windswept runway, but couldn't leave the plane until all the potatoes were unloaded. The sacks were hauled into a waiting truck and taken to a storage building before the potatoes froze in the minus-32-degree temperature. I did my best to keep warm while several mine employees, wearing heavy insulated clothing, unloaded the potatoes. Finally, after about twenty minutes, I was allowed to jump out onto the ice where I was met by a cold wind and a warm handshake from a mine supervisor. Charlie was welcomed with a pat on the head.

The supervisor took us to a large equipment shed where Charlie and all our gear would spend the night.

Some of my gear had been knocked off the sled when a heavy box fell sideways onto it during the unloading of the plane. After I accounted for each item, I decided I would repack in the morning so that Charlie could settle down sooner. The supervisor assured me that someone would feed Charlie with meat from the kitchen and he would be safe in the shed. I hated to leave him. He was already a part of me. The equipment shed was two hundred yards from the living quarters and once inside I wouldn't be allowed to venture out by myself because of the high winds, cold—and polar bears. I was astonished at the rules, considering the journey I was about to begin. However, it made sense to take precautions, so I said nothing and allowed myself to be led away with a last long look at Charlie before we shut the door.

My accommodations in a spacious building, constructed of strong orange-colored ribbed steel to withstand the Arctic cold and powerful winds, were warm, modern, and comfortable. The cafeteria offered generous portions of a wide variety of foods, and after eating a substantial dinner of meat, vegetables, and, of course, potatoes, I finished off with a large serving of cherry pie. I thought about Charlie alone in that dark shed. My motherly instincts were showing, but I was assured that someone had fed him and given him a good-night pat. After meeting and talking with some of the mine personnel, I went to my room and took a long hot shower, which I knew would be my last for a month, and went to bed.

I spent a restless night thinking of the long, lonely journey ahead. I thought, too, about the family and friends I had left behind, hoping my journey wouldn't worry them too much. Bill and my parents were supportive, I knew, but in the dark hours of the night I wondered what their innermost thoughts really were and whether for my sake they were masking their concern for my safety. It was too late to turn back now. I had worked and planned for this journey for the past two years.

When I could no longer sleep, I rose and got dressed. The cafeteria opened at six, so I went down for breakfast. Mindful that this would be my last meal in civilization, I piled my plate high with sausages and eggs. Just as I was about to take a mouthful, Don Souter, whose job at the mine was to keep polar bears at a safe distance, announced in a cheerful voice that there was a polar bear and her two cubs out on the ice close to my starting point. Pulling on an enormous jacket, he told me not to worry. "We'll chase them away with the snowmobiles." As he left, he took my appetite with him. My stomach went into a nervous frenzy, rebelling at the thought of food.

Although I had been thorough in my training and learned all I could about polar bears from the Inuit, I had yet to face one in the wild. My route to the pole would take me through a region with a large population of polar bears. How would I react in an encounter with one of these potentially dangerous nomads? Leaving my breakfast, I walked over to a large, double-glass window, overlooking the bay where I was to begin my journey in two and a half hours. The scene stretching before me was totally white and I saw a powerful beauty that matched the power and sheer size of the polar bears that call the frozen Arctic home. I couldn't see any bears, so I returned to the table and made a reasonable effort to eat, although my heart wasn't in it. I hid my fear beneath a laughing, joking exterior so that the people who were waiting to see me off wouldn't know that I was scared to death.

At 7:00 A.M., I made my last call to Bill. I knew that

he would keep in touch with Bezal and Terry by phone throughout my journey, sending messages that would be relayed to me by radio. But this was the last time we would be able to speak together. He knew that this was the moment of my departure and he was waiting at the helicopter hangar in Florida for my call.

I was so afraid of the polar bears I might face that I began to cry when I heard his voice. I told him of my fear and he tried to reassure me. "After all," he said, "there's no guarantee that you'll actually meet a bear."

That made some sense and I stopped crying. One part of me still wanted to turn and run home, but an even bigger part wanted to go to the pole and deal with whatever challenges lay ahead, even polar bears. If I went home now, I would be quitting on myself and would have the rest of my life to live with that thought.

After talking to Bill, I called Terry at Resolute Bay to tell her I would soon be leaving and would radio her at 8:00 P.M. with my new location. Then I dressed in my warm expedition clothing and went to the equipment shed to see how Charlie had spent the night. Without a care in the world, he was up and happy to see me. Tim Sewell, one of the mine employees, walked over from behind some equipment and told me that he worked on night shift. He had come in last night, turned on the light, and was immediately confronted by a large, black dog, which stood there quietly watching him. After he recovered from his fright, he called by intercom to the main building to report that there was a big, black dog in the building. He was told that it was Charlie and why he was there.

Tim, a dog lover, told me, "I patted him and he looked so lonely I decided to feed him something special. I rounded up some of my buddies and we went to the kitchen, got us a bucket of meat, and took it back to Charlie. He ate it in record time. Then we gathered up all the old coveralls we could find and made a soft bed for him. You sure have a great dog there. Take care of him."

My sled load was a bigger mess than I had thought. I had unpacked some equipment at Resolute Bay and tied it to the outside of the sled bag so that the sled could fit in and around the other freight on the plane. But when the heavy box fell on the sled it had broken the main tie-down rope and sent things flying. Now I looked at a mixed-up heap with gloves sticking out of a food bag, a spare hat on top of the stove, and all sorts of supplies in odd places where people the night before had stuck them so that they wouldn't be blown away when we got off the plane.

I was really upset. I have always been finicky about details and in particular about putting things in certain places and keeping to an organized plan on expeditions so that if something goes wrong, as it occasionally does, it's much easier to deal with the problem. As I began to sort things out and repack, several people hurried to help, stuffing objects into places they thought they should go. They created bedlam and my load was still a mess. They were well-meaning and enthusiastic and I didn't have the heart to say, "No, don't do that." It was so much easier to say, "Thank you," and pull the zipper shut thinking that I would rearrange the load that night in camp. I realized later that those who have the ability to say "no" have a precious gift. It was my first lesson of the expedition and I hadn't even started yet.

I pulled my loaded sled out the door and down to where the frozen land met the sea ice. Charlie was at my side, harnessed to his sled and leashed to my waist belt, sitting patiently on his haunches, wondering, I supposed, what was going to happen. The date was March 30, 1988, and we were ready to leave on the most challenging journey of our lives.

2.

THREE BEARS

DAY 1

≡ I pushed my leather ski boots into the bindings of my skis, clipped the heel cables shut, and was ready to step out onto the sea ice when two Inuit suddenly appeared. They announced that the bear and cubs Don had spoken of earlier had been spotted close by, hidden in the rough ice directly along my path. One bear was enough, but mother bears with cubs are known to be particularly hostile and aggressive. Once again my mind was numbed with dread but I forced myself to finish putting on my skis, doing my best to conceal my fear from the dozen people from the mine who waited at the edge of the sea ice to see me off.

It was already 9:00 A.M., a cold, sunny, clear day, and I wanted to take advantage of the weather to ski as many miles as possible. After last-minute photos and good-byes, I stepped from the ice-covered land onto the glistening white blanket of ice covering the black waters of Crozier Strait between the east coast of Bathurst Island and the west coast of Little Cornwallis Island. Straining to look into the distance, I could see no sign of the bear and her cubs in that vast white expanse. That, I thought ruefully, is why polar bears are white.

The first quarter mile of shoreline was a rough mass of icy pinnacles, some jutting upward ten feet high, broken and jumbled by the persistent rise and fall of the tides that sigh and groan beneath the great weight they lift. After a few yards I realized it was too rough to ski. I laid my skis on top of the sled and began to pull it by hand through the narrow gaps in the ice. Then I went back to help Charlie pull his sled.

I kept pulling and tugging, searching ahead for gaps wide enough to pull my sled through without jamming. Still in sight of the mine, I noticed with relief that my well-wishers were beginning to return to their jobs. I had hoped to begin my expedition with a grand, dashing start, skiing off into the distance in impressive style. Instead, the ice seemed to be doing its best to make my forward progress slow and difficult.

A few more yards of pulling and tugging and I could see where the jumbled shoreline ice met the sea ice. Ten more feet and Charlie and I were through. I was rewarded by the glorious sight of smooth, white, shimmering ice, streaked with ridges up to six inches high called sastrugi and separated by patches of hard-packed snow. Once on the smoother ice I donned my skis and sled harness, checked Charlie's harness, and skied off pulling my sled, sliding easily over the ice. Charlie was having no problems pulling his sled either.

The clear sunny day combined with the smooth ice was a perfect way to begin my long journey. But I couldn't make the dread and fear of meeting a polar bear go away. I kept thinking of Bill's reassuring words, trying to drain all the comfort I could from them. Then, suddenly, I stopped at the sound of an approaching snowmobile. Don, followed by a cloud of snow dust, caught up with me and said that although they had seen the tracks of the bear and her two cubs, they had been unable to find them. "We saw their tracks going north into the shoreline ice," he said. "It looks as though they're hidden in the rough stuff somewhere ahead of you." Then, wishing me a safe journey and reminding me to keep a careful watch for bears, he drove back to the mine, leaving Charlie and me alone.

As I turned once again to ski north, I shut the door on civilization. I knew I would see no other humans for a month. I would be entirely alone in this cold, wind-swept, empty place. But there was no time to think about that. Now I knew the bear and her cubs were still close by, I had to be watchful. On one hand, I dreaded my first encounter with a bear, but on the other, I knew I would eventually have to face one, so I might as well get it over and done with. Only then would I know for sure if I had the courage to stand my ground.

As I skied I had an eerie feeling of being watched. I tried to see in all directions at once. Every few minutes I stopped to look left to right and behind me, trying to pick out any shapes or movement that would warn me of a bear. At least in this area of smooth ice I had clear visibility.

I skied on with Charlie walking at my right side, his

chain attached to the padded waist belt of my sled harness. He looked comfortable striding across the ice, his thick, black coat shinning in the sun. This was his home, and after all, he had already seen many polar bears and knew how to deal with them. I kept an anxious eye on him for any sign of a warning. I began talking aloud to him to reassure myself. "Charlie, I have never been so scared in all my life. I'm depending on you to warn me if a bear comes our way." I wondered if he knew how afraid I was? What did he think of being out here with a human who had yet to see her first polar bear in the wild?

In 1975, when I won the United States national luge championship, I experienced real fear as I rode my sled down an icy, narrow chute at sixty miles per hour with no brakes. There were only two ways to stop. I could race through the finish line safely or crash. Fortunately, I had more safe finishes than crashes, and the fear of a luger can be eliminated by good technique and quick reactions—a very different situation from my present predicament. As far as polar bears were concerned, I was food. They don't care about the refinements of technique and reaction time.

I knew that, in spite of all the questions I had asked the Inuit and the careful instructions they had given me, I still had to learn to live with the uncertainties of sharing this icy world with polar bears. But I couldn't allow my fears to overpower me. Polar bears are clever, silent, powerful predators at the top of the food chain with no need to fear man. I kept the rifle lying on top of my sled, loaded and ready for use. But the last thing I wanted to do was shoot a polar bear. Perhaps I might only wound him, which would leave me with not only a hungry bear, but a hungry, angry bear, which is even worse.

The Inuit had warned me to shoot a bear only as a last resort because a wounded polar bear is unpredictable and can turn into a killing machine in an instant.

Although I had used firearms while growing up in New Zealand and I had practiced at home with the Winchester, I was not a hunter. Alongside my Winchester I kept my eight-inch orange flare pistol ready to distract approaching bears. I had practiced using that too, but I felt my best defense against marauding bears would be Charlie.

A light ten-mile-per-hour wind drifted in from the north. At 32 degrees below zero it was stinging cold on my face and I stopped to put on my dark-blue neoprene face mask. The cloudless blue sky, made pale by the reflecting ice, stretched for miles to the west across Bathurst Island, to the east across Little Cornwallis Island, and north up Crozier Strait. After leaving the Polaris mine, I planned to ski northwest on the sea ice, six miles across Crozier Strait, to about half a mile off the east coast of Bathurst, turn north following the Bathurst coastline all the way to the island's northern shores, then, turning northwest, ski to Sherard Osborn Island. From there I would continue northwest to the northernmost corner of the west coast of King Christian Island, which would be my most northerly reference point, then travel south thirty miles to 77 degrees 26 minutes north latitude and 102 degrees 43 minutes west longitude, the area south of King Christian Island that was the estimated location of the approximate center of the magnetic North Pole in the spring of 1988.

So that I could positively identify my position when I arrived at King Christian, I had decided to travel the entire length of the west coast of the island all the way to the northwest corner, identifying the various geographic features of the coast along the way. Although my most northerly point would be thirty miles north of the pole, my journey up the coast would allow me to identify the island and enable me to easily locate the pole position to the south, and I would also be able to gather more photographs and other educational information for the school program.

After arriving at the pole, I would travel to my prearranged pickup point, skiing a rough triangular course throughout the pole area, touching on islands to the east, north, and south. Then I would fly back to base camp. I intended to navigate with the aid of maps, a twenty-four-hour sun compass, and an experimental Global Positioning System unit. I planned to ski and walk, depending on ice conditions, over the sea ice all the way to the pole through a maze of islands. Because the land is covered by a layer of wind-blasted frozen gravel, which showed itself through the patchy ice, skis and sled runners would soon be destroyed on land.

I spent the next four hours skiing at a steady pace, stopping every two hours for a hot cup of a high-carbohydrate liquid from my thermos, followed by a handful of high-fat butter crackers and peanut butter chocolate candies. At each stop I fed Charlie a handful of dry dog food from his sled, but he was more interested in my crackers and candy. I gave him two crackers at each meal but no peanut butter cups. Inuit dogs are used to a diet of seal meat and I didn't want to make him sick on strange foods, especially chocolate. "Charlie, my food isn't good for you," I told him at our first stop. "You can have a few crackers but no candy." He was not at all interested in that explanation. After gobbling up his two crackers, he stood waiting for more. I felt guilty and I turned my back so I didn't have to see the begging look on his face. That didn't work. He just walked around to face me again. "No, Charlie," I told him, "you have to trust that I know what's best for you." I wondered how long my willpower would last.

Skiing kept me warm but it was too cold to stop for more than ten minutes at a time. When I stopped the head wind that had slowly increased with the day seeped through my insulated clothing to my core, despite the windbreaker I wore for traveling. At the second stop, I grabbed my big down parka and put it on. It fitted me like a small sleeping bag, making me look like the Michelin man, but it provided the extra warmth I needed.

The ice-covered sea I was skiing across had been named after Captain F. R. M. Crozier of the ill-fated 1845 Franklin expedition, which left no survivors. The ships used in many of those early expeditions were crushed by the moving ice pack and often sank with loss of life, sometimes leaving no trace of ship or crew. The Franklin expedition was one of tragedy, but the Arctic also had many tales of survival. Naturally, I hoped mine would be one of them.

At two o'clock I arrived at a spot about half a mile off the coast of Bathurst Island. I turned directly north and began the long journey up the coast, which, as I looked ahead of me, seemed to stretch forever. I thought of the pole. It seemed such a long way off. There were at least another 340 miles to go and goodness knows how many polar bears. My progress during the first five hours had been disappointing because I had spent so much time watching for bears. I had to find a way to keep careful watch and still make good time.

Charlie and I had crossed the tracks of the female bear and her two cubs four or five times but as yet had seen no other sign of them. We had also crossed a set of much larger bear tracks, probably a male's. I had looked over my shoulder so often since setting out in the morning that I said aloud to Charlie, "I would probably do better if I turned around and went backward to the pole."

We had also seen tiny, delicate Arctic fox tracks crisscrossing the bear tracks, but no sign of the owners. The foxes, with long bushy tails and winter coats of dense white fur, follow polar bears out onto the ice pack to scavenge leftovers from seal kills. On land, they eat lemmings, tiny rodents that live on the Arctic islands.

The Bathurst coastline stretched ahead to my left. The ice-covered, rounded hills sloped in a gentle curve down to icy beaches where land and sea ice met. The gleaming whiteness of the ice obliterated all boundaries between sea and land ice, leaving little visible difference between the two at the shore edge. My map, which I kept in the upper left pocket of my windbreaker, was to become an important tool from now on. To keep track of where I was, I marked every detail of the islands on the map as I passed by. River mouths, hills, and inlets would be the most obvious landmarks. But up ahead, the barren land appeared to be fairly featureless. According to my map the highest point here was only one hundred feet and that was farther inland.

Bathurst is a large island, with an area of about ten thousand square miles, located in the central area of the Queen Elizabeth Islands of Canada's Northwest Territories. In 1819 the explorer William Edward Parry named the island for the English principal secretary of state, the earl of Bathurst. Far above the tree line, the island is devoid of trees and is generally low-lying with no mountain ranges. In the northern part of the island some inland peaks rise over nine hundred feet, but most throughout the island are less than three hundred feet. The coastline is irregular with long inlets that stretch far inland. Bathurst belongs to a vast empty area of icy, dry polar desert, which begins south of Resolute Bay and stretches all the way to the geographic North Pole at the top of the world. The cold, dry Arctic air causes an absence of snow-producing clouds, so the snowfall is usually less than a few inches per year. The snow is fine-grained, dry, and abrasive.

The afternoon wore on as the sun swung south, then west, still with no sightings of polar bears, only tracks that made my heartbeat quicken and my skis go faster to get away. At 6:00 P.M. the sun dropped over Bathurst. With its disappearance the temperature plunged thirteen degrees in the next hour to minus 45 degrees Fahrenheit and the wind, which had gradually increased throughout the day, was a steady twenty-five miles per hour by seven o'clock, kicking snow into the air. I had traveled eleven miles so I decided to camp about four hundred yards offshore. The ice had lost its sunlit sparkle and was bathed in a cold, gray, moody light that subdued the definition of the sastrugi ridges.

Once I had stopped, I grew colder by the minute, and I quickly slid into the warm, bulky depths of my down parka. To generate body heat and provide shelter from the wind I hurried to set up camp. But first I took a hollow metal ice screw from a small, blue nylon bag on my sled where I kept all of Charlie's gear, his spare chain, collar, and fabric booties, in case he cut a foot on the sharp ice. I twisted the ice screw down into the ice and attached Charlie's chain to it with a metal caribiner. After a few minutes of hunting on his sled for his feed dish, I finally found it where someone had put it on my sled. Filling the dish with dry dog food, I set it in front of him. Charlie was eating even before my hand left the dish.

The time spent searching for gear and handling metal objects made my hands ache with cold. Some fingers were already almost numb. My thin pair of liner gloves under medium-weight outer gloves weren't enough to prevent frozen fingers. I had to find my insulated mitts fast. Although too large and bulky for finger dexterity, they provided extra warmth. They should have been in the front of the sled under my down parka. They weren't there. That morning's repacking fiasco was beginning to make itself felt. But it was too late to look back and think about what should have been done. I had to find those mitts. Someone must have put them in my clothing bag, which would seem the logical thing to do. The bag was buried under the radio and sleeping bag but now my fingers were numb and white. I stood windmilling my arms as fast as possible to pump blood into my frozen fingers. It had no effect. I needed the mitts. The cold dry air and wind chill of minus 100 degrees was drawing the last heat from my hands.

I finally found the clothing bag and grabbed the zipper, fumbling with fingers that felt like wooden blocks. I jerked the zipper open, but where were the gloves? There was no time for an organized search. I dumped everything onto the ice and the mitts tumbled out. I grabbed them, plunging my hands into them. Frantically windmilling my arms again, I tried to pump blood into my fingers to keep frostbite at bay.

It took at least ten minutes before I felt the first effects of my efforts. Then the searing hot pain of returning circulation began. But at least the agony in my fingers told me they were still alive. Frostbite could leave my hands useless and this was only the first day of my journey. Jumping up and down and running in tight circles, I kept the warming process going. I didn't dare look at Charlie. I could only imagine what was going through his mind at the sight of all my frantic activity. Finally my hands were acceptably warm and the hot agony in my fingers was bearable.

Frostbite is a constant worry of climbers on high mountains and even at lower elevations. Once, on Mount McKinley, I suffered very mild frostbite while climbing at over twenty thousand feet. But the dryness of the Arctic air pulled the warmth from my body faster than anything I had ever experienced. Handling cold metal objects would require extra care. So with painful, barely functional hands, I put up my blue nylon tent, anchored it to the ice with six ice screws, and unloaded my red down sleeping bag, two foam sleeping mats, clothing, stove, and a one-quart bottle of white gas stove fuel. I put everything neatly in my tent, my sleeping gear on the right-hand side, clothing and cooking gear on the left. I laid the nylon bag containing three extra thermometers, a wind gauge, a data log book, pencils, and journal on top of my sleeping bag ready to enter the day's events.

As I set up my tent I looked around for bears. Charlie was staked out twenty feet in front of the tent, giving him good visibility with time to warn me of any sign of an approaching bear. But I couldn't resist checking, even if only to satisfy my nerves, which had been stretched tight all day. I needed something warm to eat and drink, but I knew that once I lit my stove it would sound like a blowtorch and prevent me from hearing anything over its roar. It would be up to Charlie to bear-watch while I cooked. But there he was curled up on the ice apparently asleep. Not very reassuring. I wanted him to keep at least one eye open for bears, and I walked over to wake him up. As I called his name he looked up for a moment, then promptly tucked his nose somewhere under his big furry tail.

I looked down at Charlie sleeping and realized that trust was going to become a major part of this expedition. He had lived in polar bear country all his life, and trying to control everything about Charlie and my surroundings would drain my energy. I obviously had to leave some things to Charlie's judgment. Still, it was hard to turn my back on Charlie and light that noisy stove. The trust I needed wasn't going to come in one easy step.

I knelt in the tent doorway bending over the stove, but my painful fingers couldn't push the tube leading from the stove into the gasket at the top of the fuel bottle. After a few minutes I gave up. Instead of rice, potato flakes, milk powder, and butter, followed by hot chocolate and crackers, I chose crackers, peanut butter cups, and granola mixed with milk powder. It was rather dry but quite good. I finished the meal with the only cup of hot water I had left from my day's supply, mixed with chocolate powder. A meal fit for a queen.

It was almost eight o'clock, the scheduled time for my first radio call to base camp. I anchored my radio antenna to the ice with a sharp stake and ran the antenna through the binding of one ski, which was standing on end next to my tent. Then I suddenly realized I had forgotten to warm my nine D cell radio batteries. I kept them in a small green stuff sack in my sled, and a pocket in the upper part of my bib pants was perfect for warming them. But time was running out. It was two minutes before eight. I couldn't be late calling in on my first night. I shoved the batteries quickly down the neck of my clothing, leaving only one thin layer of fabric next to my skin. I reasoned that being so close to my body they should warm up right away. In a moment I realized my mistake. The one layer of fabric wasn't enough to stop the freezing batteries from burning my skin. They came out of there with the speed of lightning.

Now I had only one minute left before radio time. I held the batteries in my gloved hands just inside my jacket. At 8:10, with a short prayer, I put them in my radio and turned it on. It sprang to life. I pressed the transmitter button and said, "Kiwi expedition calling eight-one-five Resolute. Over." The cheerful voice of Terry Jesudason replied, "Eight-one-five Resolute to Kiwi expedition, where are you? Over." I gave her my exact location, weather conditions, and number of miles traveled that day.

"Did you see any bears?" Terry asked. When I said "no" I could hear the relief in her voice as she replied, "Good. I hope you don't meet any." After about five minutes, I said good night from Charlie and me and closed down. My radio conversations had to be brief to conserve battery energy, which is quickly sapped by the cold. This was only my first night so they had to last a long time yet.

I was tempted to climb into my sleeping bag, but first I had to repack my sled, no matter what my tender hands were trying to tell me. I unloaded everything into the tent so that nothing would blow away in the persistent wind. I kept the heavier items—radio, food, and fuel—on the bottom of the sled, with lighter objects on top and my day food bag, vacuum bottles, camera, and extra warm clothes for stopping and emergencies in the front within easy reach. Finally all was a picture of neatness. My sled was tied to the left-hand ice screw at the front of the tent, my skis were laid alongside the tent so they wouldn't scoot along the ice in the wind, the shovel was just inside the tent vestibule, and Charlie's sled was tied to the right-hand ice screw with his load of dog food cinched down tight. My rifle was within easy reach at the tent door. Even with a wind chill of minus 100 degrees and throbbing hands, I couldn't help stepping back to survey the tidy scene with real satisfaction. I was back to my organized self. Now I could think about sleep.

Before climbing into my sleeping bag I checked Charlie. He looked comfortable, but it bothered me that he was sleeping on the ice without anything under him. Taking a brown gunny sack that was wrapped around his dog food, I tried to push it under him, but one eye came up from the bushy tail with such a reproachful look that I stopped. Tony told me that Charlie had slept on the snow and ice all his life and didn't mind it. Now I had the distinct impression that he preferred it and was wishing I would stop fussing and let him sleep. It was another lesson on leaving some things to Charlie's judgment.

After a last look around for polar bears, I checked the temperature, still minus 45 degrees. At least it wasn't getting any colder. Then with throbbing hands and gritted teeth, I eased off my boots and jacket and climbed into my sleeping bag. I was settling down into the cozy depths when I remembered that I hadn't brushed my teeth. There was no way I was going to get out of this warm bag now. Besides, I remembered I had no water left. The perfect excuse.

I lay looking at the tent roof and walls, wondering how long it would take a bear to rip through the two layers of thin nylon. The answer, of course, was almost no time at all, and the thought made me cringe. But even as all sorts of terrifying pictures flew through my mind, I decided that I would have to discipline my mind against thinking about polar bears while I lay helpless in my sleeping bag. I needed a good night's sleep before another long day. With a giant emotional hand I pushed all negative thoughts aside and forced myself to relax. I was in good physical condition from all my training and the day's skiing hadn't tired me. Except for my hands and polar bear nerves, I felt very good. I checked that the rifle and flare pistol were close by my side, then called out to Charlie, "Good night," and fell asleep.

DAY 2

I woke at 5:30 A.M. after a restless night's sleep. My hands were blistered clubs and hurt every time I touched something. Overnight enormous blood blisters had formed to reach all the way down to the second joint of each finger except my left little finger, which had somehow escaped freezing. I knew I had to keep the blisters intact so that my hands wouldn't become raw and bleeding. It would be better to use my heavy mitts as much as possible even though they were clumsy. I thought back to the previous morning, remembering the crazy repacking of my sled with gear ending up in all the wrong places as I just stood there not wanting to offend anyone. I decided what is done is done. One learns one's lessons the hard way sometimes and, besides, if that was to be the only problem of the whole expedition, then I would consider myself lucky.

Reaching over I painfully and slowly unzipped the tent door to inspect the new day. Just like yesterday. The wind had dropped. I looked out at cold, clear skies and a light northerly wind. Another beautiful Arctic day. Charlie was up and looking at his empty bowl. I crawled out of my sleeping bag, creating a minor snowstorm as I brushed against the frost-covered tent roof while I pulled on my jacket. I'm normally a morning person but there was something about the intense cold, the tent frost down my neck, and my sore hands that made that morning most unappealing. But it was time to greet Charlie and start the day.

Stepping out of the tent, still in my insulated blue camp booties, I checked the thermometer, minus 41 degrees. I looked around for bears or tracks and saw none, but I was surprised to notice that the shore ice with its jagged blocks and pinnacles ended only one hundred feet from my tent. In the settling light of last evening it had looked as if I was at least four hundred yards from the closest rough shore ice. It was my first lesson in the sly nature of the changing Arctic light and the way it affected depth perception.

Charlie was bouncing up and down at the end of his chain looking well rested. I hugged him good morning as his soft tongue wiped across my face. I poured what looked like a pound of dog food into his bowl, which he attacked with gusto.

Now for my stove. I simply had to light it that morning. I needed water for the next leg of my journey and a hot breakfast would get my day started off right. I carefully put a pair of woollen gloves over my liners and with clenched teeth I forced my cruelly protesting fingers to push the stove tube into the gasket at the top of the fuel bottle. Success. I lit it, put snow and ice into my two-quart pan, and soon had warm water. To conserve fuel, I heated water only to a temperature at which I could still put my finger into it.

It was only six o'clock, so I decided to have a leisurely breakfast of a bowl of granola, milk powder, coconut flakes, raisins, and butter mixed with warm water. I sat on my sled to enjoy the full effect of my first breakfast of the expedition only to find that after the third spoonful it was frozen. So much for leisurely breakfasts! I added more warm water and ate the rest as fast as possible. Then I melted enough ice to fill two vacuum bottles with water and a carbohydrate powder.

The dry Arctic air holds little moisture, causing quick dehydration of the body, which, in turn, causes early fatigue and reduces the body's ability to keep warm, so fluid would be just as important as food to keep my energy reserves up. I put my day's supply of crackers, cashews, walnuts, and peanut butter cups in my day food bag along with the two vacuum bottles and slipped everything down into the front of the sled bag. Then, remembering Charlie's appetite for crackers, I added a few more.

Last to be packed was the tent. I was completely engrossed in finding a way to twist the tent ice screws out of the ice so that my hands wouldn't scream in protest when suddenly I heard a deep, long growl coming from the depths of Charlie's throat. In a flash I looked at him and then in the direction in which he was staring. I knew what I would see even before I looked. A polar bear!

It was a female followed by two cubs coming from Bathurst Island, slowly, purposefully, plodding through the rough shore ice toward me. They were two hundred yards away. With a pounding heart I grabbed my loaded rifle and flare gun and carefully walked sideways a few steps to Charlie, who was snarling with a savagery that caught my breath. Without taking my eyes off the bear,

I unclipped Charlie from his ice anchor and, again walking sideways, I led him to the sled where I clipped his chain to a tie-down rope. The bear, now only 150 yards away, wasn't stopping. Her cubs had dropped back but she came on with a steady measured stride while I frantically tried to remember all the Inuit had told me. Keep eye contact, move sideways or slightly forward, never backward, stay calm, don't show fear, stand beside a tent, sled, or other large object to make my five feet three inches appear as large as possible. Don't shoot unless forced to. Don't wound a bear, you'll make it even more dangerous, and never run. Repeating to myself, "Stay calm, stay calm," I fired a warning shot to the bear's left. The loud explosion of the .338 had no effect. On she came. I fired a flare, landing it a little to her right. Her head moved slightly in its direction but she didn't stop. I fired another flare, this time dropping it right in front of her. She stopped, looked at the flare burning a bright red on the white ice, then looked at me. She was only one hundred feet away now.

By this time my nerves were as tight as violin strings and my heart could have been heard at base camp. The bear began to step around the flare, and I dropped another flare two feet in front of her. Again she stopped, looked at the flare and at me. Then she fixed her tiny black eyes on Charlie, who was straining at the end of his chain, snapping and snarling trying to reach her. She looked back at her cubs. I could sense her concern about Charlie's snarling, rabid act and her cubs. She waited for her cubs to catch up, then moved to my left in a half circle. In spite of my sore fingers I fired two more flares in quick succession, trying to draw a line between her and me. She stopped, then moved back toward my right. I fired two more flares and again she stopped. She seemed to want to cross the line of flares but was unsure of the result and of Charlie, so she elected to stay back. She kept moving right in a half circle, still one hundred feet away. Finally, with a last long look she plodded north with her two new cubs trotting behind her, their snow-white coats contrasting with their mother's creamy, pale yellow color.

The whole episode lasted fifteen minutes but seemed years long. I was a nervous wreck. My hands were shaking as I stood still holding my rifle and flare gun, watching the trio slowly move north. But in spite of the mind-numbing fear that still gripped me, I could feel deep down inside a real satisfaction. I now knew that I could stand up to a bear in the wild, stay calm enough to function and still remember the words of wisdom from the Inuit. With Charlie's help I had passed my first test. The bear had been completely silent as it had approached and moved around me on paws thickly padded with fur on the undersides. I was thankful for Charlie's warning. Now he had stopped growling and snarling but still stood rigid, watching the bears as they zigzagged in and out of the rough ice hunting for the seals that lived in the cold waters beneath the ice. He seemed to hardly notice the giant hug I gave him. He was still on guard.

The bears were only about four hundred yards away but I decided to continue packing my tent and move around to stay warm, still keeping a wary eye on the bears. I was getting cold. My fear and flowing adrenaline had kept me warm but I was beginning to shiver now. I finished packing and stood around until ten o'clock, keeping warm, until I was sure the bears had disappeared and weren't circling back to me. If I stayed out from the coast, keeping away from the rough ice, I hoped to make up the time I had lost. But as I started out I still thought about the bears. Even as frightened as

I had been, it was a thrill to see a bear and her cubs in their natural environment. She was unafraid of me, powerful and dangerous, yet graceful. And she was a tender, attentive mother caring for her cubs.

All went well for the next hour. As usual I tried to look for bears in all directions at once. Being alone, I had to keep a 360-degree watch. The sky was still clear with just a light wind coming from the north. It was bitterly cold and my blue neoprene mask was developing a thick layer of ice where my breath froze. I could see Kalivik Island two miles northeast. I should be well past the island by nightfall.

Suddenly I noticed movement about four hundred yards away to the southeast. Surely not another bear. My nerves weren't yet ready for a second encounter. But a moment later there was no doubt. It was a bear. It was downwind from us, and Charlie hadn't picked up its scent. As fast as I could, I released my skis, again grabbed my rifle and flare gun, and attached Charlie to the sled rope. I stood waiting with Charlie at my side. He was watching, his body rigid and his back hair standing on end, eyes fixed on the approaching bear, but he was silent. In a voice that was anything but calm, I said, "Why don't you growl? Do something, Charlie." But then I sensed that his silence was a signal to me. He knew something that I didn't know. So I, too, stood silent, watching, not moving, with only the sound of my pounding heart in my ears.

This bear was a very large, powerful male, the same creamy white as the first bear, and he was moving toward us at a faster pace. His head was held low and he walked with a typical polar bear pigeon-toed gait. He stopped to raise his black nose, his head moving slowly back and forth as he caught our scent, then he lowered his head and walked on again. Charlie was at the end of his chain, still silent, except for an occasional short, low growl. Then as the bear came to within 250 feet, Charlie fell completely silent again. There was something different about this bear and he knew it.

The Inuit had warned me not to show fear. But I couldn't just stand there and tell myself I wasn't afraid. I was terrified. So I tried replacing my fear with aggressive thoughts. "I have as much right to be here as this bear," I said to myself. "He has no right to invade my space." It sounded ridiculous but it worked. Instead of shrinking to a defensive position, I began to feel that I had at least some control over the situation.

Now the bear was only 150 feet away. I fired one warning shot to the left, then two flares in quick succession. He kept coming toward me, very deliberate and more aggressive in his movements than the first bear. I quickly fired three more flares, each one landing in front of him. He veered to the left, then turned to face me. Just as I fired another flare, he started forward faster than before. I quickly reached for Charlie's collar to release him. It was time for Charlie to use his bear-chasing skills.

My thumb was on the collar clip when Charlie suddenly leaped three feet in the air at the end of his chain with a loud snarling growl that set my right eardrum ringing. The bear stopped in his tracks, took one long look and, as I fired more flares, slowly retreated to our left. Charlie was once again silent. So I took the cue and stood silently at his side. I watched as the bear moved away in a wide sweeping arc, looking back over his shoulder now and then. He had been impressed by Charlie's leaping attack and was leaving reluctantly. My worry now was whether he would return.

Sure enough, at about three hundred yards he stopped and turned to face us. He paused for a few moments as if contemplating the situation, then started back with the same quick, determined pigeon-toed walk as before. This was too much. The pit of my stomach was an ice cube, even my knees were shaking. We had to get rid of this bear somehow, but I was undecided about whether to let Charlie go so he could deal with the bear or to try to shoot to kill.

The bear was still two hundred yards away, so I decided to fire a last warning shot and flares before taking more drastic action. I fired the .338 but I could tell by now that these bears were not very impressed by the loud cannonlike explosion, so I began laying out flares as fast as I could, thankful that I had bought a supply large enough to do an army proud. All at once the bear bent down and touched a hot, burning flare with his nose. He threw his head in the air, rolled on the ice, got up as quickly as a cat, then moved out as fast as he had arrived. It was with heartfelt relief that I stood watching him disappear. He didn't even bother to look over his shoulder this time.

After two encounters with bears in one day, I needed to stop to regroup and have something to eat and drink. I had a severe case of the shakes and I was beginning to wonder if my nerves could stand much more of this abuse.

I hugged Charlie long and hard. He had helped me twice in one day. "Thank you, Charlie," I said. I fed him some crackers, and as I ate my share I wondered again at the different moods Charlie had shown when facing these two bears. There was much for me to learn out here. Tony had been right when he told me to keep Charlie tethered until I needed him to chase a bear. That way I had control over him and he would be there at the precise moment I needed him. Charlie was leaning on my leg begging for more crackers. I didn't have much appetite. I felt as if I had just survived a head-on collision with a freight train. I gave Charlie my crackers. He had no problem with his appetite. This polar bear business was fun to him.

So far I had traveled only two miles. It was 1:00 P.M., cold and clear, time to move on again. I was opposite the southern tip of Kalivik Island, a low-lying, ice-covered island with a high point of only 176 feet and a sloping shoreline that blended in with the sea ice. I could see rough ice ahead where the currents rushed through the narrow channel between Kalivik and Bathurst, causing the ice to pile up. I headed on a course midway between the islands hoping to find thick, stable ice.

I slowly put my skis and sled harness on and checked Charlie's harness and sled. All was ready to go but I still felt emotionally drained and jittery. I dreaded entering the area of rough ice only three hundred yards ahead of us. The mounds and pinnacles would be perfect cover for a bear. I had heard many stories of polar bears stealthily, silently stalking people who had no idea they were there until they were attacked. I laid a hand on Charlie's broad back to bolster my courage. He walked with alert confidence, his head up, looking ahead. Here was an animal born and raised amid all this snow and ice, and he knew instinctively what was going on around him. I was a visitor who had to learn to survive in this environment or risk destroying myself by making mistakes.

Quite soon I was entering a forest of icy pinnacles, mounds, and blocks, which surrounded me, reaching over my head, some as high as fifteen feet. The only sounds were occasional tired, low groans or a long-drawn-out tortured squeak as the edges of the ice pack pushed past each other. Sometimes a loud crack like a rifle shot from deep within the ice pack would jar my frayed nerves. I zigzagged back and forth on my skis, then found it easier to walk as I searched for a path through the icy forest.

It was a beautiful place. I stopped to photograph ice towers leaning at angles in defiance of gravity and wide blocks of ice as large as garages, some with caves scooped out in their sides. There were streaks and layers of pale blue, so delicate and fragile looking that I reached out to touch the sculptured smoothness of the icy walls. I had come upon a treasure chest of beauty I had never before imagined. I walked on, my earlier fright and worry stripped away, replaced by exhilaration and awe at my icy surroundings. The meteorological office at Resolute Bay had told me before I left that satellite photos showed rough ice. Every year brings changes in the ice pack. Fall and early winter storms affect the way the ice sets up. Some years it is quite smooth but this year it was rough, which brought travel problems and could hide polar bears. But it also brought a beauty that made me glad I was there.

After an hour of walking through the maze, I hadn't made a lot of progress. I had stopped so often to look, feel, and photograph that I decided to take a short break to eat and drink. Charlie and I enjoyed crackers and peanut butter cups together. He had persuaded me that a few peanut butter cups wouldn't hurt him. His method was simple: just sit and stare at her as she eats each mouthful, she will eventually give in. I also gave him a handful of dog food and I ate a few walnuts. Charlie didn't like walnuts and I was thankful to be able to eat something without his black eyes looking at me reproachfully. There was no doubt in his mind that if he stared intently into my face for long enough I would share my food. And, of course, he was right. My will power hadn't even lasted a day.

After our break I walked on, weaving back and forth, the path always opening in the right places. Walking at my side, Charlie suddenly fixed his attention on an area two hundred feet to the front and a little to the right of us. He stopped, growling that same warning growl I had heard before. He stepped in front of me to the end of his chain as if to protect me. I needed no further warning. I went through the routine I had been through twice before that day. I clipped Charlie to the sled, grabbed the loaded rifle and flare gun, and stood waiting, my heart pounding against my ribs.

There was a slight movement to the left of a garage-sized block of ice but I couldn't be sure. Charlie was looking in that direction so I was certain the bear was in front of us. I kept watching ahead and keeping an eye on Charlie, depending on him to warn me of the bear's direction. Suddenly, there it was, about 175 feet ahead. It looked like a medium-sized male, not as large as the last bear. It stood still, staring at us. I took the offensive early. I fired a warning shot and several flares while Charlie snarled and went berserk at the end of his chain. The bear stepped back and raised his black nose in the air. But we were downwind of him, so he circled wide to the left, moving in and out of the ice to get to where he could catch our scent and find out what we were.

Charlie and I turned to face the bear as it circled to our rear. I had some anxious moments when I lost sight of him behind large chunks of ice but he always reappeared. Almost directly behind us now, he stopped and again raised his nose. This time he would be able to catch our scent. Would it tell him we were food or would he decide to leave us alone? I fired a few more flares and after the bear had taken a long look at Charlie's rabid act, he turned and slowly ambled off to the south and rear of us. Now I had to decide if I should walk ahead and take the risk of the bear returning and sneaking up on us from the rear. He would be downwind and Charlie wouldn't pick up his scent. But this bear seemed to be more curious than aggressive so I bet on his leaving us alone.

As I began to walk ahead, I kept imagining the bear creeping up behind us. I went as fast as I could, trying to put as much distance as possible between us. To save time I tossed glances over my shoulder rather than stopping to look back. Then after about twenty minutes Charlie leaped with a snarl to the end of his chain out to our right, almost pulling me off my feet. I saw number-three bear fifty feet away. He had returned and was almost level with us. I fired four or five flares as fast as I could. The bear moved farther out and continued in a wide circle to our front, then to our left, and back to our rear. It stopped and took two steps forward. I quickly fired more flares and the bear, which still seemed to be only curious, turned and ambled away as if glad to be rid of us. It might have surprised him to know the feeling was mutual.

I was emotionally exhausted. Three bears in one day was too much. If I had to deal with them every day in these numbers, I really doubted that I could survive the journey. The chance of meeting that one bear that would stop at nothing and force me to play my last card would increase with the number of encounters. Before we stopped for the night, I decided to travel until I could find an area of ice where I wasn't completely hemmed in on all sides and Charlie would have reasonable visibility and be able to warn me of an approaching bear.

Ahead and over to the east, I could see a smooth ice

floe that had escaped most of the grinding and crushing forces of the ice pack. I stopped in the middle and looked about. This would do. Charlie had clear visibility for at least two hundred yards in all directions. I settled him for the night with his pan full of dog food and placed his sled so that it would protect him from the drifting cold north wind. It was a little warmer than last night. The thermometer read minus 41 degrees Fahrenheit. It was close to five o'clock and the sun was beginning to slide down over the western edge of Bathurst Island. I had traveled only three miles this long, difficult day.

I had my warm down parka on and was doing my best to work with my big mitts on. My hands were protesting and throbbing as I put my tent up and prepared camp. But my hands weren't my main concern just now. My mood was despondent. I felt down, a very unusual feeling for me. I'm more often accused of being overly optimistic. Tonight I would have to deal with my feelings. I would have to decide whether I could continue. These bears were scaring me out of my wits.

I melted ice and poured warm water over rice, potato flakes, soup mix, and butter. I had a dessert of peanut butter cups followed by two cups of hot chocolate. As I ate and drank, sitting on my sled sheltered behind my tent, I thought about my predicament. I had trained hard and sacrificed much for this expedition. It was a challenge of a lifetime and I wanted to succeed. It is one thing to be a member of an expedition of several people, but very different and infinitely more difficult to travel a journey like this alone, on foot. There is no one else to hold the other end of the tent so that it doesn't blow away. No one to share camp chores. No one to talk to about fears. No one to help make decisions, and, above all, no one to help watch for bears.

The questions I had to answer were, Will I meet this many bears every day? If I do, will I survive? Do I have the courage to continue through this mind-wrenching fear for days on end? Can I do this alone? I knew beyond a doubt that the Inuit were right. I was far more vulnerable to bear attacks traveling at a slower pace on foot and alone than I would have been had I gone by faster dogsled.

But then I reasoned that, although I was traveling through a heavily populated polar bear area, the fact that polar bears are solitary animals made it unlikely that I would meet so many every day.

The bears I had met that day had come from different directions. Each was alone, each had acted differently, and I had survived. It seemed that if the numbers were reduced, and even if I met even two or three more, my chance of survival should be good.

Rifle shots sounded too much like the cracking sounds that came from deep within the ice pack, and, therefore, weren't much use as a warning, but the flare gun was invaluable. And, of course, there was Charlie. He was indispensable. He had a sense that told him how each bear should be treated and his savagery was something to behold. Charlie was a powerful bundle of muscle and in that savage mood I had no doubt he could take care of himself. Tony had told me, "A dog can't win a head-to-head fight with a polar bear but a clever dog like Charlie knows how to nip a polar bear's rear legs and at the same time keep away from his powerful jaws and claws."

As I sat there putting the pieces of the puzzle together objectively, I could see light at the end of the tunnel of fear. My first job was to conquer my fear and replace it with aggression so that I could stay under control, do whatever I had to do when confronted with danger. I had to trust Charlie and the advice I had been given by the Inuit. As I looked back over the day, I realized that I had made no mistakes and I hadn't panicked. At least I had passed that test. But I knew it would be wise to keep to the tactic of letting Charlie off his chain only when a bear appeared likely to charge. I had to sense that moment just before the charge to give Charlie time to do his job. Furthermore, Charlie would be safer that way. Tony had told me that he would charge after a bear any time he saw one. If I let him off his chain every time a bear appeared, his chance of being hurt would increase many times over.

And, of course, there was the ultimate deterrent: shoot to kill. It was a repugnant thought as I sat there picturing such a scene. I'm not a hunter, although legally I could kill a bear in self-defense, in which case, according to the law, I would have to radio base camp immediately and the wildlife people would fly out to inspect the bear and take the skin. I was confident of my skill with the .338 but I was now convinced that I would have been better advised to carry a shotgun. At home when I had listened to the confusing and conflicting pieces of advice given me by hunters, it seemed that a .338 Winchester had won out. Now I realized that I should have asked people who had dealt with polar bears on the same footing as I was dealing with them. But after further thought, I came to the conclusion I didn't know anyone who had done just what I was doing.

A .338 would be fine as a hunting weapon but not as self-defense against a close-in charging bear. One bullet from the .338 would have to get by that massive bone structure and hit a vital spot right on target, whereas a shotgun, with its wider shot pattern, would cover a larger area of a charging bear. I thought back to the man who had told me to "just shoot the bear in the neck." That might work if I could find the neck. Another felt that a "single shot in the eye would do the trick." But if that man stood only a few feet from a bear and looked into those tiny dark eyes, I wondered, would he change his mind? I wondered what the fear factor would do to anyone who thought he had all the answers. If I succeeded in wounding a bear, my fate could be sealed. Many an Inuit has been killed by a wounded bear. And above all, killing a polar bear in its own territory was something I still felt I needed to avoid. I thought about the two cubs trotting behind their mother trusting her to protect them. Killing a bear like that would leave two orphans. What would happen to them?

Now I felt more confident. I had thought the problem of survival through and felt that my tactics were the right ones. I would react to each problem as it arrived, let Charlie go at the precise moment if that moment arrived, and shoot to kill only as a last resort. I said a short prayer of thanks for my family and friends, for all those people in the climbing world and their patience in teaching me over the years what I needed to know, and for the Inuit who had taught me the art of Arctic survival. But above all I was thankful for my beloved Charlie.

I decided to continue. This expedition was survivable. Optimism flowed through my veins again. I hurried over to Charlie, woke him up, and gave him a huge hug. I was crying. The frustrations of this difficult day were gone and the tears flowed in relief. Then a strange thing happened. My eyelids froze shut. The cold had turned my tears to ice. Now I had to thaw my eyelids open. I had just learned another lesson. There could be no more crying on this expedition.

I gradually thawed my eyelids with warm saliva and it occurred to me that this would not be a good time for a visit from a polar bear. It was a painful job to gradually scrape and thaw the ice away. Fifteen minutes later I could see again.

I went back to Charlie and sat on his sled. He leaned on me, laying his big black head on my knee. I stroked his silky black ears and talked to him about my thoughts and plans for the days ahead. After a few minutes I heard the gentlest of snores. Charlie had fallen asleep on my lap. I looked at my watch. It was 7:30, almost time for the radio call to base camp. I left Charlie curled up behind his sled, sound asleep. I warmed the radio batteries, placed them in the slots in the back of the radio, and turned it on. It instantly crackled to life. I called base camp and reported my new position to Terry. I briefly mentioned the three bears and assured her that Charlie and I were fine and ready for tomorrow.

I climbed into my sleeping bag thankful to be alive. It had been the most terrifying day of my life. I felt exhausted but sleep didn't come. The sun had long disappeared over Bathurst Island. The cold, gray light of the Arctic night lay over my camp. The wind had left and the ice was silent. My ears were straining for any sound that would tell me of an approaching bear. At eleven o'clock a light dusk settled over Charlie and me, like a gray blanket. It was still almost light enough to read a newspaper. Twenty-four-hour daylit days were fast approaching. At 2:00 A.M. the gray blanket began to lift, replaced by the pale, soft gray of early morning. Still listening for bears, I drifted off into an uneasy, restless sleep.

3.

POLAR BEAR

PASS

DAY 3

≡ At 6:00 A.M. I was awake but not rested. It had been a tense night listening for bears. Charlie had made no sound and I hadn't heard the dreaded sound of a bear. As I lay in my sleeping bag trying to persuade my reluctant body to move out of the tent into the cold to begin a new day, I thought about yesterday. But my mind rebelled and I resolved not to dwell on the past. No more thinking of the yesterdays, they were gone. Instead I would save my emotional energy to think and plan ahead. I needed to travel as many miles a day as possible to move quickly through this heavily populated polar bear area. Having set a firm course of action in my mind I crawled out of my warm sleeping bag into the bleak cold of the early Arctic morning.

My first job was to take stock of my hands. The blood blisters were larger and redder than yesterday and both hands were more swollen. My usually large hands were now very large and certainly weren't candidates for a beauty contest. There was no sign of infection. Surely no self-respecting bacteria would live in this cold place, I thought, as I gritted my teeth and squeezed my swollen hands into blue liner gloves that now seemed two sizes too small.

I unzipped the tent door, grabbed my warm parka, and stepped outside. I looked quickly around for bears while I walked across the ice in my camp booties, sliding into my jacket as I went. Charlie had just got up and was stretching and yawning. I hugged him good morning. "Did you sleep OK, Charlie?" A lick across my face with his big soft tongue told me "yes."

The first long golden rays of the new day's sun were already washing over the tent, turning the tiny ice crystals covering the blue nylon into dancing, sparkling diamonds. I fumbled around trying to make my hands cooperate so I could light the stove. The pain in the tips of my fingers made that out of the question. I had to devise a method of using the palms of my hands and my wrists to connect the fuel bottle to the stove. With some patience it worked. The stove roared to life as loudly as a blowtorch and I moved to where I could see Charlie in case he warned me of a bear. It was impossible for me to hear anything over the roar of the stove. I quickly put a pan of ice on the stove to melt while I fed Charlie. I was in a hurry to leave this place and find smooth ice again with better visibility. It was spooky in this icy forest.

The water was barely warm when I poured it over my granola. I ate fast, then gulped down one cup of hot chocolate and began packing my sled as more ice melted to fill my thermoses. In another forty-five minutes all was packed and Charlie and I were ready to leave.

The rough ice stretched ahead as far as I could see but it was possible to ski around the mounds now. Charlie and I zigzagged back and forth, finding narrow gaps between the pillars of ice, which allowed our sleds to slide through without jamming. Suddenly Charlie let out a blood-curdling yelp. I almost had a heart attack. I thought a bear had got me. Then I realized I had stepped on his front paw with my ski. He stood holding his foot up and I stopped and rubbed it to make sure it wasn't cut. "I'm sorry, Charlie," I said. Then miraculously it was instantly well. Amazing what a little attention can achieve.

Another hour went by and I could see about half a mile ahead to where the maze of pillars appeared to end at a long east-to-west ridge of ice. It was a ten-mile pressure ridge, stretching snakelike all the way from Bathurst Island to Kalivik Island, about ten feet high with some peaks reaching fifteen feet. Pressure ridges form when the leading edges of two ice floes or bodies of ice meet, coming together under tremendous pressure, crumpling and grinding upward to form rough, jumbled, jagged ridges. Sometimes the pressure is forced downward, creating a pressure ridge beneath the water. I hadn't expected to find a ridge of this size in this area, but the ice pack is unpredictable and changes every year. I was halfway between the two islands. Here, the ridge appeared to be at its highest. Away off in the distance it was lower closer to Bathurst and Kalivik. But it was a long way to ski to the lower ends. Perhaps I could find a gap close by.

The tracks of a large polar bear and the tiny tracks of an Arctic fox crossed our path. They looked only a few hours old. I couldn't see any sign of the owners so I nervously kept going. Charlie exuberantly pressed his black nose hard down on the ice over the bear paw prints and tried to follow them. I yanked his chain as hard as I could with my right hand to stop him from pulling me off after the bear. It developed into a tug-of-war. I gained ground after shouting, "No, Charlie," and, "Come here, Charlie," several times. He conceded victory, but he gave me a long sideways look that told me I hadn't won any points for imagination. My unsportsmanlike conduct in not joining in the bear chase was clearly not appreciated. "Charlie, we're supposed to avoid bears," I said, "not look for them."

At a hundred feet away I still couldn't see any real gaps but there were snowdrifts built like ramps on the side of the ridge. Over to the left I spotted a small cave that had been lived in, but was now smashed inward. Bear and fox tracks ran everywhere. I saw a large splotch of blood and a mostly devoured seal three feet in front of the cave. Charlie was gleefully trying to pull me over there, so I gave in and joined the investigation. It had been a ringed seal breathing hole, which had drifted over with blowing snow to form a cave, with the unfortunate occupant having met a violent end.

Seals are the polar bear's main food source. The ringed seal, so called because of the pale rings on a dark skin, is the most common seal in the area. They live in the sea under the ice and come up for air through breathing holes in the ice pack, usually in cracks or in the thinner ice. During the winter when the ice becomes hard and thick, they have to keep their breathing holes open by constant scratching with the strong, curved claws of their fore flippers. Blowing snow drifts over the hole, camouflaging it. The snow becomes deep and hard-packed enough for the female seal to excavate a small snow cave or birth lair, in which she has her pup in the spring.

The snow cave is supposed to protect the seal and her pup from the prying eyes of a hungry polar bear. But polar bears have a remarkable sense of smell, and they can detect ringed seal breathing holes beneath a layer of snow as much as two or three feet deep. When a bear senses a seal breathing hole or birth lair, it smashes it with massive front paws and in a flash grabs the unfortunate seal or pup. The thick layer of fat beneath the seal's skin is the polar bear's favorite meal. Arctic foxes commonly follow polar bears to scavenge the leftovers of the hunt. By the looks of this scene a bear and a fox had eaten well.

Charlie was having a picnic scratching and chewing the bloodstained ice and eating a few scraps of leftover seal. When he tried to roll in the blood I decided enough was enough. A dog that smells like a seal might become an attraction instead of a deterrent to polar bears. There were probably more seal breathing holes around the pressure ridge, undoubtedly good hunting for polar bears, in which case this was definitely a place I wanted to leave as soon as possible.

To our right was a promising-looking ramp of hard-packed snow reaching halfway up the pressure ridge. On each side of the ramp the tortured, fractured ice was piled in an uneven mass of jumbled blocks, some six feet or more across. Leaving my skis beside my sled and using my ice axe for balance, I climbed the ramp looking for a way over the top. At the top four feet of unstable broken ice still had to be crossed. The only thing to do was chop a path over the top, pull my sled up, then lower it carefully down the other side.

After twenty minutes of chopping I formed a usable path. Climbing back down I tied a fifty-foot piece of seven-millimeter rope onto the front handle of my sled; then, grabbing the sturdy handle, I pulled it up the ramp. Now for the tricky part. Holding on to the sled with one hand and balancing myself so that I didn't end up at the bottom of the ramp again, I tied the rope around a three-foot block of ice. Then, carefully stepping around the sled, I got behind it ready to push it over the top. Suddenly, my feet shot out from under me and I somersaulted down the slope to land right under the nose of an astonished Charlie, who jumped back in alarm. Unhurt, I scrambled to my feet thinking dire thoughts about pressure ridges and sleds. Climbing up again, more carefully this time, I pushed the sled over the top, then slowly lowered it with the rope down the other side. Now for Charlie's smaller, lighter sled. It was quite easy to pull up and over, using the same system.

The pillars of ice were behind us now; ahead lay a smooth stretch of terrain. But as I was standing on top of the ridge, I noticed strange-looking bumps in the ice about half a mile out. It was 11:30 A.M. when I started off in that direction. The sky was still clear and the wind speed read twelve miles per hour. The temperature had lowered to 33 below zero, sending the wind chill to 60 degrees below zero. My face mask was covered with an inch-thick layer of ice that molded the mask to the shape of my face. My eyelashes were frozen. I was growing tired of looking at the world through a row of miniature icicles that hung down in front of my eyes. At first I tried to rub them off but each time an icicle came off, it brought with it an eyelash. The thought of returning to civilization with no eyelashes made me stop rubbing. Even out here by myself in the middle of this icy desert, vanity was still a factor.

I was anxious to reach the icy, dark bumps I had seen ahead of us. My curiosity was soon satisfied. I stood looking in disbelief across a sea of ice that looked as if it had boiled into giant bubbles, each bubble a solid mound of ice six feet across, two feet high, frozen in place. The snow had been swept away, leaving a smooth, shiny, dark blue-green surface with thin strips and circles of hard-packed snow around the mounds. It was old, multiyear ice, perhaps twenty feet thick, rock hard, worn smooth by the wind and sun, with the salt and air squeezed out.

The synthetic skins that I had started out with were still on my skis. They performed well, giving my skis the extra grip I needed to pull my sled. But these shiny smooth mounds would be a real test. Charlie had had no problem with traction so far, but I wondered how his feet would grip the hard, bare ice ahead of us.

We had already passed Kalivik Island. I could see nothing but mounds of ice to the east so I decided to angle west, closer to Bathurst, in search of a way around the strange mounds. At first I kept to the packed snow bordering the edges of each mound, trying to find extra grip for my skis. After spending hours weaving through the rough ice we had just left behind, I longed to ski straight ahead and make good time. I decided to tackle the mounds.

By standing solidly on the middle of my skis to gain all the grip I could, I managed to walk my skis up one side of a mound, then slide down the other with my sled teetering on the top before it came flying crazily down the slope, catching the tails of my skis. Meanwhile, Charlie was following at my side at the end of his chain. I was concentrating so completely on staying upright and dodging my flying sled that at first I didn't

notice the sideways tug on Charlie's chain. Finally, he
got my attention by jerking at his chain, stepping out to
the right onto a patch of snow, and stopping. I was
thankful he couldn't put into words what was on his
mind. His eyes were gloomy and his ears drooped. His
expression told me that he was not going to put up with
these straight-ahead tactics any longer. He was having
trouble gripping the smooth ice of the mounds, and the
only way he was going to continue was to follow the
snowy edges.

I had already begun to realize that my tactics weren't
working. The flying sleds were dangerous. This was no
place for either Charlie or me to break a leg. I felt terri-
bly guilty at being so impatient and putting speed ahead
of safety. It was time to stop and put matters right with
Charlie. The best way to ask for forgiveness was with
food. Releasing my skis and sled harness, I pulled the
day's food bag out of my sled. Sitting on his sled with
my arm around him, I fed him crackers and a few peanut
butter cups. I told him, "I'm sorry," and patted his head
as he ate. His gloomy look was immediately replaced
with his begging look. Everything was all right between
us again. I managed to eat a few peanut butter cups
before he finished the entire day's supply.

On we went, pulling our sleds, following the snowy
edges around the mounds as we gradually angled over
toward Bathurst Island. I had already marked Kalivik
Island to the east off my map, and now I could see
Goodsir Inlet on Bathurst. The coast was still very low,
and according to my map the inlet appeared to be almost at sea level for about a mile inland. The map also
showed a river mouth there, but it was frozen and impossible to see in the afternoon's white glare. I was a
mile offshore and still angling in.

The glare was a problem. As the afternoon wore on, I squinted more and more, trying to see through the bright reflected light for landmarks and bears. My double lens goggles were a nuisance. They kept fogging up and the fog quickly turned to ice. When I used the mountaineering trick of wiping saliva on the inside of the lens, it too instantly froze and had to be scraped off. The goggles were not the wrap-around kind and seriously inhibited my peripheral vision. They made me feel as if my world was closing in around me, and the thought that there might be a bear just around the corner where I couldn't see it drove me to distraction. But every time I tried to do without the goggles I could feel my eyes burning in the bright light and I was forced to put them back on. This was only day three and once again the polar bears were making me ride the fine line of survival. I reminded myself that only emotional discipline was going to get me to the pole.

About four hours after we first entered the ice mounds, they began to decrease, replaced with longer areas of packed snow. I was less than a half mile off the Bathurst shoreline, in the transition zone between the rough fractured shore ice and the older, thicker sea ice. Before I turned directly north up the coast, I checked the measuring wheel that was attached to the back of my sled. Each revolution of the metal wheel moved a counter that gave me the number of miles I had traveled. It was already four-thirty and today's mileage, so far, totaled only five. All that work for so little gain.

To make matters worse I could see more rough ice ahead. This area was supposed to be smooth—at least those were the reports from last year. I was the only expedition to travel to the magnetic North Pole this season so I hadn't been able to get any current ice conditions except for a report from the meteorological office and two of Bradley's pilots who had told me, "The ice seems to be more broken and pressured this year along Bathurst." So far they were right. Bezal at base camp had also warned me that the ice might be rougher this year. He was just as concerned about wind. He called the route to the magnetic North Pole a wind tunnel. As yet wind had not been of any significance. Perhaps I would be lucky for the entire journey. I decided to travel two more miles, then camp. My mask was cold and beginning to freeze to my face. Even so it still protected my skin from the cold wind.

I reached another pressure ridge, this one only three or four feet high with long easy gaps between the blocks of ice. "This is more our size, Charlie," I said with pleasure. But on the other side all I could see was a field of broken, jumbled ice stretching north, east, and west. The sun, low in the sky over Bathurst, was spreading a golden glow over the western sides of tall pinnacles of ice that cast long, dark, ghostlike shadows to the east. A fog of ice crystals, turned golden by the setting sun, was also spreading softly over the low coast of Bathurst. The scene before me was unreal, unearthly. A photograph could never capture the cold, naked beauty of a land and icescape untouched and uncomplicated by man.

Standing there beside Charlie, I was afraid to go through those silent, dark shadows that lay across our path. I wouldn't see a polar bear in there until he was too close. A feeling of vulnerability swept over me and thoughts of Bill sprang into my mind. He knew about the three bears yesterday and he would be worried about us. To add to my fears, Charlie had been sniffing the air to the east for the last half hour. I could see nothing, but did he know something was out there? As I stood leaning on my ski poles looking ahead to the shadows we must pass through, I spoke to Charlie, talking away my fears. "This is spooky, Charlie, but to get to the pole we have to cross through here. A few bears and a few shadows shouldn't stop us."

The sound of my voice bolstered my courage. I put my arms around Charlie and hugged him tight. Those shadows ahead didn't seem nearly as ominous now. It was time to go and we entered the first long shadows. It was still spooky, but I was in control again.

I kept going until we had passed through the shadowed area. Meanwhile, Charlie was still looking due east. He had me worried. What was he looking for? If there was a bear out there, it must be keeping abreast of us. Perhaps it was a fox. I decided that until proven otherwise it would be a fox. That was easier for my mind to handle.

There were a few smooth ice pans, some two or three hundred feet wide, between the leaning towers and blocks of ice. An iceberg, thirty feet high, lay ahead. It came from a distant glacier and stood trapped in the crushing grasp of the ice pack, a prisoner until the summer thaw. There was a wide apron of smooth ice around it, a good camping spot with good visibility.

The sun had slipped away and the temperature was dropping, although still only in the minus thirties. The extreme dryness of the air made it seem colder. I eased my face mask off without tearing my skin underneath. It was a cold, frozen lump. Tonight I would have to thaw my mask and fix my jacket. Ice crystals had built up between the jacket lining and the outside fabric. My arms could hardly bend because of the ice. It had become a straitjacket.

I went to work feeding Charlie, making camp, and cooking and eating dinner. But he was still uneasy. He ate a little dog food but left the rest in his bowl as he stood looking into the distance to the east. Something was bothering him. Even after the long day he wouldn't sit or lie down. I arranged my skis, axe, and spare ski poles in a circle fifty feet out from the tent. My theory was that a bear might be curious enough to stop to examine these strange objects before investigating the contents of the tent. The idea was just a little silly, because if a bear got that close, Charlie would have a fit and would warn me. However, it was a psychological help.

In my tent I kept an eye on Charlie while I thawed my mask over the stove, which sat in the doorway. The jacket was next. It had a hood and was made of a red-and-black windproof fabric with a zipper all the way down the front. There was a thick layer of ice along the zipper that thawed out in a cloud of steam that froze almost instantly into ice crystals and formed a frozen fog inside the tent. During the day the zipper kept freezing up and jamming. Now as I pried it open I had to be careful the zipper teeth didn't break. I found the jacket could almost stand up by itself because of the thick layer of ice between the lining and the shell. The lining was sewn shut so I slit the sleeve endings to allow the ice to fall out as soon as it formed. It looked a little ragged but would now be much more functional. It was a good traveling jacket. But when I stopped, I always put my big down jacket over the top of my clothing in an effort to keep the cold from creeping in. The down jacket was too bulky and warm to ski in.

At eight o'clock I called base camp to give Terry my position and sent a message to Bill. Terry told me Bill had telephoned and sent his love. These daily messages relayed by radio and telephone were a comfort that I looked forward to. When I signed off I noticed that Charlie was still standing guard. Sleep was out of the question for me until I found out what was out there. Wearing my big down parka, I sat on my sled, facing Charlie, with the rifle and flare gun close at hand, and wrote in my journal. The pen had frozen, so I took out one of the many pencils I had brought with me. My hands made writing difficult. As I held the pencil between the inside edges of my index and middle fingers, my usually bad writing was made worse, but it was important to write details of the events and my thoughts for the day. "After experiencing such awful mind-consuming fear continuously for three days," I wrote, "I wonder if the real definition of courage is the ability to deal successfully with one's fears. At the end of this expedition I hope to be not only alive, but also able to say that I have courage."

Suddenly Charlie growled softly. Dropping the journal, I grabbed the rifle and flare pistol and moved quickly to his side. I squinted through the gray light but could see nothing. Charlie growled louder. Then I saw a movement to the side of a small car-sized block of ice. It was an adult bear standing about two hundred yards away, looking straight at us. Charlie was motionless and quiet. I stood still and waited. When the bear began to walk toward us, Charlie sprang to life with a fierce snarling growl. The bear immediately backed up and, seemingly satisfied, Charlie stopped growling. The bear, still two hundred yards away, moved to the south of us, then stopped, as if to come forward again. Charlie was ready with another ear-tingling snarl. The bear appeared to think better of the whole situation and left, moving at a fast lope, going south. I guessed it had been following us some distance off to the east for several hours. Charlie apparently knew it was there but sensed that the bear was just curious and only growled when it took the liberty of moving toward us.

I was relieved beyond words and again thankful for Charlie. He was relaxed now and went about eating his dinner. He seemed satisfied that another bear episode was over. I gave him a good night hug just before he curled up to sleep. How I wished I could figure out these bears the way he did. He obviously could sense the difference between an aggressive, dangerous bear and one that was only curious. It was eleven o'clock. The pale light of a full moon sparkled across the ice. I felt confident that we had seen the last of the curious bear, so I climbed into my sleeping bag for my best night's sleep on the ice so far.

DAY 4

Six A.M. and everything was still. It was cold but clear. I was fortunate to have begun my journey during a period of high pressure. It brought cold temperatures and light head winds, but also gave me good visibility. The nearby iceberg looked like a medieval castle in the early morning light. Its sides were smooth, while its top was a crest of jagged spires. It had a forlorn, lonely look, as if it had wandered away from its neighbors and found itself trapped, unable to return.

I was growing accustomed to the changing Arctic light and its various effects on the surrounding ice. The evening shadows were soft at first as they settled silently over the ice, then dimmed to a cold, harsh gray, to be replaced by the early morning's soft, golden glow, which changed into the harsh glare of midday. I stood there, the only human amid the ever-changing beauty of the Arctic. But as beautiful as it was, I felt very small and alone in a space that seemed endless in all directions.

I sat on Charlie's sled, my map on my knee, discussing the day's plan with him. He sat on the ice in front of me, loudly crunching his dog food, appearing not to really care about my map and plans. An hour later all was packed and we were on our way. Today I hoped to find an easy path through the ice to reach at least as far as Black Point, which was on the edge of Goodsir Inlet. It was eleven miles away and would put me in a good position to cross the fifteen-mile inlet tomorrow in clear weather. Halfway across I would have to pass Polar Bear Pass, an area known for polar bears. "If you're still going when you get to Polar Bear Pass," the Inuit had warned me, "you can expect trouble this time of the year around there and to the north and south of the pass." Considering that I had already had more than enough trouble from bears, I couldn't wait to put the area behind me. The very name of the place made me nervous. I resolved not to think of it until tomorrow.

Soon I was about half a mile off the eastern shore of Bathurst. I couldn't see any improvement in the ice to the east so I decided to go straight ahead and hope that it would be easier later. We crossed several bear tracks. Some were large but one was gigantic, almost a foot across. I told Charlie, "I hope we don't meet the bear that fits into these tracks."

Now and then Charlie stopped to dig frantically straight down into the ice. His front paws were like backhoes. Whenever we passed over seal breathing holes concealed by a thick layer of snow, Charlie could smell them with his sensitive nose and wanted to investigate. I spoiled his fun by insisting we keep going. The last thing I had time for was excavating seal holes. We passed a few open holes where the ice had broken apart, leaving cracks that froze over with thinner ice, making it easier for a seal to maintain a breathing hole. One such hole was surrounded by bear tracks. I wondered if the seal had escaped in time.

There were numerous Arctic fox tracks. I saw several foxes, each one alone, skittering quickly and nervously in and out of the blocks of ice, keeping its head and body low with its fine, white fur coat and long bushy tail held out behind it. Arctic foxes were a beautiful sight. Their little pointed faces seemed too delicate for such a harsh place. Sometimes they stopped briefly to look Charlie and me over, then silently disappeared behind the ice. I'm sure we were being watched more often than I realized. Charlie displayed only a mild interest in the foxes. He would much rather find a polar bear. Being more faint of heart, I found the foxes to be quite enough.

As the morning wore on, the wind increased to fifteen miles per hour, coming from the north straight into my face. Dry, fine, sandy snow was blowing toward us, sliding over the ice, staying low and not affecting visibility. My eyelashes were covered with the usual icicles and my mask rapidly iced up, but I was learning to accept these things as normal.

By now, on day four of the expedition, I was finding it impossible to relate to the things I had left at home. It was becoming difficult to imagine a hot shower, a soft bed, and living in a house. My mind could no longer grasp the civilized task of shopping. Out here the only task was my emotional and physical survival. I had become completely one with my new environment. This, coupled with the concentrated effort I needed to continually watch for bears and plan so that I didn't make any fatal mistakes, left no room for any other life. I was also fast losing my sense of time. To combat that, I stopped every so often and said aloud the date, the time from my watch, and the day number of the expedition. Verbalizing time placed it back into my awareness, and I resolved to go through this ritual every morning as I started out so that my sense of time would remain intact. I had had no warning of these psychological changes, but I took them as a good sign that I was totally engrossed with survival, in which case I could expect to survive.

The ice hadn't improved. It was difficult to pick out the low-lying landmarks on the shore of Bathurst to my left. I was making good progress, according to the mileage counter wheel on the back of my sled. It was only noon and it already read seven miles. Then I began to have doubts. I could see a point of land extending from the coast of the island with a frozen river mouth in the middle. But the river I was looking at on the map was only half the distance along the coast that the mileage counter indicated I had already traveled. I couldn't tell which one was right, the map or the counter. I hoped it was the counter.

I skied on, looking for more landmarks through the white glare. The jagged teeth of the sharp wind bit into my body, even though the sun shone. At ten miles I decided to gain a better view toward the east, hoping to find smoother ice. I was heartily sick of the rough, jumbled blocks. My pace was slow and frustrating and I was confused about how far away Black Point really was.

The coast of Bathurst rose over one hundred feet in elevation, making it a good place for a better view of my surroundings. I veered in that direction, and the ice became thinner and crossed with cracks, creaking and settling as I skied over its uneven surface. I headed toward a likely looking snowy ramp leading up from the sea ice onto the ice-covered land. Hooking Charlie to the back of my sled, I pulled it up the ramp by hand, while he pulled his sled behind me.

At the top of the ramp, about fifty feet up, there was a wide, level ledge. Ahead was another rise of about seventy-five feet to another, even wider ledge. The knifing wind blew stronger the higher I went. In order to spend as little time in the stronger wind as possible, I decided to leave Charlie with the two sleds while I hurried up the slope to get a better view. I had only gone five yards when I was stopped in my tracks by a loud, mournful howl. Charlie was upset that I was leaving him. I couldn't take another howl like that and felt guilty that he was so unhappy. So I unclipped his chain and we hurried off together. Delighted, he jumped all over me and rolled on the ice. He knocked me down twice. I picked myself up and said, "Charlie, I think I've had all the joy I can stand." We bounded up the slope, Charlie out in front at the end of his chain, and my right arm, which was attached to the chain, stretched like elastic.

On top of the ledge I was greeted by a glorious sight. There, a quarter of a mile ahead, was Black Point and beyond I could see right across Goodsir Inlet. I had skied and walked twelve miles and was relieved to find that the distance shown on the wheel counter was right. The river I had seen on the map was much closer to Black Point than I thought.

I looked to the east and north for smoother ice. The

sterile, rocky land I stood on had wide patches of frozen, sharp gravel, which would make it impossible to haul my sled across the island.

I saw that I had to move out about a mile offshore to where the sea ice appeared to have longer stretches of smooth pans between the jumbled areas.

It was too cold and windy to stay any longer on the ledge so Charlie and I returned to the sleds. I slid them both backward down the slope onto the sea ice again. By now it was 3:00 P.M. and I had grown cold in the increasing wind. I didn't want to start across the inlet this late in the day. I preferred to start in the morning and push hard to reach the other side in one day. I skied northeast until I was a mile offshore. It would be a good starting place for tomorrow. The ice was still rough, but the jagged piles were only about two or three feet high and spread out, making visibility possible for Charlie during his bear watch that night.

I made camp and discovered my evening and morning chores were becoming routine. My fingers hadn't improved and remained very painful. The dark-red blisters were still intact and really looked grotesque. But there was no infection and I hoped they would improve with time.

After dinner I sat in my sleeping bag writing in my journal. Polar Bear Pass jumped into my mind. "How glad I will be to be past this place," I wrote. "We crossed at least eight sets of tracks today, each one making my heart race. Charlie loves to find tracks and would like to explore each set to find the owner. Polar bears are the most magnificent animals I have ever seen, but just now I hope I never see another one in my life. This is the first expedition where at times I have had cause to wonder if I will survive. But of course I have no option but to survive. There is Bill, Mother, and Dad, and, of course, I must take Charlie home."

I lay back in my sleeping bag and thought about Bill and my parents. Their love and friendship was especially important to me now. I looked forward to taking Charlie home and showing him off as a new addition to my family. I had grown to love him and knew everyone else would fall under his spell. I hoped our other three dogs wouldn't mind this big black boss dog taking over. I knew Charlie's nature would accept no position other than first.

Finally I pushed away thoughts of my family. This was no place to become homesick. I knew perfectly well that on a solo expedition such as this where I felt as if I was traveling through "Polar Bear City," downtown, at rush hour, I had to think only thoughts that were good for me. All others had to be ignored. With polar bears for company, crossing Polar Bear Pass and beyond to the pole, I reminded myself again that emotional control was essential to my survival. It would have made such a difference to have someone to talk to and help watch for bears. But then my sense of reality took over and I said aloud, "The facts are, I'm alone, I'm on foot. I'll deal with things as they come." With that said, I felt more relaxed and optimistic.

I decided to visit Charlie once more before bedtime. I walked over to him, calling his name. He raised his head briefly, opened his sleepy eyes, then dropped his head back down and tucked his nose under his tail. "Well," I thought, "not much conversation here, I might as well go to sleep myself." I patted him good night and went back to my tent.

The wind had dropped. It was a clear evening and I marveled again at my good fortune with the weather. It

looked good for tomorrow, too. Before turning in I decided on one last visit to the "restroom." Considering
the lack of such amenities and the temperature, I relied
on zippers in strategic places and, of course, speed was
of the essence. At least privacy was no problem.

DAY 5

≡ Today from my camp at Black Point I hoped to
travel fifteen miles across Goodsir Inlet to Rapid Point.
Nine miles deep by fifteen miles wide, Goodsir Inlet cuts
into the eastern shore of Bathurst Island. And to reach
Rapid Point I had to cross the outlet of Polar Bear Pass,
a wide, low-lying valley stretching about twenty miles
between the western and eastern shores of Bathurst,
dividing the island into unequal north and south sections. The floor of the long, sheltered valley averages
only ninety feet above sea level. Many streams and rivers flow from the rolling hills on each side of the valley
into the large Goodsir River, which, during the summer
thaw, flows swiftly eastward into Goodsir Inlet. The
sheltered valley is home to a variety of Arctic animals,
including denning female polar bears and their cubs,
musk-ox, Peary caribou, lemmings, Arctic hare, Arctic
fox, and ermine. But in April, the river is frozen solid
and the valley is used by polar bears crossing from the
sea ice on one side of Bathurst to the sea ice on the
opposite shore. Hence the name Polar Bear Pass.

During my observation of polar bear tracks during the
first five days of my journey, I saw no tracks in areas of
multiyear ice, such as the area of frozen mounds I had
passed through on day three. However, I saw many
tracks in areas of cracked and moderately rough ice and

pressure ridges, especially around the minor ridges. No doubt the areas in which seals can maintain breathing holes dictate where the polar bears hunt in their never-ending quest for food.

The day started well. I decided to take advantage of the clear visibility and cut straight across the Inlet instead of following the coast. I found a series of ice pans, some several hundred feet wide, surrounded by rougher ice caused by the pressuring of the pan edges. When one pan ended I crossed over the rough edges to another smooth pan a few feet away. I was making good time, skirting some large mounds of ice over fifteen feet high sprinkled here and there. They were all different shapes, streaked with the now familiar tints of pale blue.

We crossed over several cracks in the ice, some only a hair's width and others perhaps six inches across. Charlie didn't like to cross the wider ones. He always hesitated but followed in response to a sharp tug on his leash. He was afraid of falling into the water. I wondered if an Arctic dog instinctively has respect for the cold, chilling waters, knowing that a dip can be fatal.

We were crossing Polar Bear Pass outlet and as I skied I remarked to Charlie, "I wish they had called this place Squirrel Pass. I could handle that." I had seen two sets of bear tracks as we set out at 7:30 in the morning. Now it was close to ten o'clock, almost time to eat. There was a larger hummock of ice ahead about twenty feet high. It looked like a small iceberg. I decided to stop to eat on the other side.

About twenty feet in front of the iceberg, Charlie stopped and began growling loudly, his back hair standing on end. I had no doubt that it was a bear. I tore my skis off, unclipped the sled ropes from my harness, grabbed the rifle and flare gun, and stood waiting with

Charlie at my side still clipped to my harness. He was at the end of his chain, snarling, staring straight at the wall of ice. Every nerve in my body was tense.

Suddenly, a full-grown male bear stepped out from behind the ice, paused momentarily, then with unbelievable speed bounded straight as an arrow for my sled. He flipped the offending object to one side with a mighty swipe of a massive front paw as if it were a tiny toothpick. I stood terrified, rooted to the spot. Charlie's growls were deafening. Then the bear, only twenty feet away, apparently saw me for the first time and partly rose up on its hind legs, dwarfing me as I stood there. The bear began to charge and I was jolted into action. My right thumb on Charlie's collar clip pressed down and instantly released him. I dropped the flare gun and raised the rifle to fire point blank at the bear as Charlie raced to its right rear leg and hung on with all the strength in his powerful black body.

As I fired, the bear dropped onto all fours and the bullet zinged harmlessly over its head. Now, its mouth open, it desperately tried to reach Charlie, but he was hanging on, twisting away from those vicious teeth. Around and around they went until, finally, the more powerful bear tore away from Charlie's grip and raced off into the distant ice with Charlie in hot pursuit.

I stood there glad to be alive, watching Charlie and the bear disappear into the distance. But my relief was short-lived. Charlie was gone. Would he come back? How could I find him? It was useless to go after him. Would the bear turn and injure him? So many questions but no answers. I was frantic. I had never been so afraid in my life, but now I felt numb. I turned my sled right side up and, still holding the rifle, sat down, praying that Charlie would come back. I walked around to keep warm, looking into the distance, hoping to see Charlie. I had no idea how long I could wait. I couldn't bring myself to think of what I would do if he didn't return. I thought about the bear. It had expressed an anger I had not seen in the previous bear encounters. It had moved swiftly and silently except for a moment before he appeared ready to charge. At that moment I was sure I detected a slight hiss from its partly open mouth.

Suddenly I saw a black spot away in the distance. Could that be Charlie? It had to be. The black spot rapidly became larger. It *was* Charlie. He was flying over the ice with long graceful strides straight toward me. I dropped the rifle and ran to greet him. We met twenty yards away in a flurry of black fur, hugs, and kisses. He was panting hard. I buried my face in his thick neck fur and wanted to cry with joy, but didn't dare. I had learned my lesson on day two when I cried and my eyelids froze shut. Instead, we returned to my sled and had a short celebration party of crackers and peanut butter cups. On the way back I picked up the rifle where I had dropped it on the ice.

I sat on my sled feeding Charlie, thinking of my encounter with the bear. It seemed to have lasted a lifetime, but couldn't have been more than five minutes, perhaps less. When I fired at the bear I felt at the time I had to use my last line of defense, but now I was thankful the bear had dropped onto all fours and the bullet missed. It was better that way. The bear was unhurt and Charlie had chased it away.

I wondered what would have happened if I had fired a single shot into the bear's chest. I knew now, beyond a doubt, that at close range it would be highly dangerous to wound a bear. This bear had demonstrated more power, anger, and speed than I could have imagined. I was surprised at the way it had reared on its hind legs. I shook my head when I thought of what little protection I had against a bear charging out from behind the ice at close range. Charlie had shown no fear. He was on his mettle. Now that he had stopped panting, he wore a big doggy smile. This was fun to him. Not for me. My hands were still shaking. The energy was drained from my body. I felt sick to my stomach.

Obviously I had chosen a bad place to stop and eat, so I gathered things up to leave. Later we went past the iceberg, where I was surprised to see a partly eaten seal lying not far from a breathing hole. The head was intact but looked crushed. The skin and fat along the back had been eaten. Apparently we had disturbed a feeding bear. No wonder he had been so angry.

Charlie chewed on the seal. I let him eat for a few minutes as a reward. Then it occurred to me that the bear might come back to finish his meal. If so, I definitely didn't want to share the same space with him again. Once was enough.

Much to Charlie's disgust I pulled him away. He tried to drag the seal with him and I imagined him thinking, "What a waste." But it was time for us to leave, as fast as possible and without Charlie's seal. We continued our journey through the pass outlet. It was almost noon and we were only halfway across. I kept looking nervously over my shoulder. I couldn't get that wild, violent scene out of my mind.

We ran out of smooth ice pans at about the middle of the inlet. During the short summer thaw, the full force of the river flows out into the center of the inlet, pushing the ice into a chaotic jumble. After another hour we were through the worst and back to the smoother pans. But the afternoon glare had settled over the ice, cutting visibility down to about a mile. Trying to see ahead to Rapid Point, I could only guess where it was. My map showed it to be a point of flat, sea-level land, about five miles ahead, that gained only one hundred feet in elevation three miles inland. There appeared to be a large river mouth there, so I could expect rough ice at the point.

I skied from one ice pan to another. In one place the ice became a smooth highway and I could see a tall, slender pillar of ice standing by itself in the far distance. It was in line with Rapid Point so I aimed for it and in no time we were alongside it. At least thirty feet high, it was white and gracefully slender. I stopped to eat and take a photo. I lined my sled and Charlie up in front of the pinnacle and set my camera on the tripod I carried with me. With the timer set I ran to stand at Charlie's side. I had my mask off and was smiling at the camera but there was no click. The camera had frozen again. The joys of Arctic photography. After a few more tries I gave up and with painful, cold fingers took Charlie's photo by himself.

At five o'clock, with the sun setting in the west, I could see Rapid Point. It was so flat I couldn't tell land ice from sea ice. I veered out around the point into a haunting, desolate, lonely moonscape. The strong sea currents swept around the point and were pulled into the inlet we had just passed. Huge plates of ice a hundred feet wide were lifted up onto each other. Some plates had ridden up over their neighbors, leaving their sharp edges pointing to the sky. As we worked our way around the point, I could only guess where the land began. The ice creaked and groaned as it protested the abuse it was being dealt from the sea currents. I kept to the less angled plates, but my skis still slid sideways to the bottom. Charlie didn't like it at all. There were too many cracks in the ice for his liking. But we kept going until the ice flattened. I didn't want to camp on the unstable ice near those swift currents and I was glad to get away from that strange, lonely, ghostly place.

It was six o'clock. It had been a long, emotionally exhausting day. More than anything, I wanted to get into my sleeping bag and go to sleep to give my mind some relief. Charlie was happy now that we had passed the broken ice of Rapid Point, but he was tired. As soon as we stopped he curled up and went to sleep even before eating his dinner.

He didn't wake up until I had set up camp, cooked dinner, and made the nightly eight o'clock base camp call. Then he was ready to eat. He enthusiastically crunched his dog food, ate three crackers for dessert, then curled up again. He, too, had had a long day. It was hard work chasing polar bears and protecting me. With a last pat and a "Good night, Charlie," I crawled into my tent, slid into my sleeping bag, and slept soundly without a single dream about bears.

4.

ARCTIC
STORM

DAY 6

≡ It was after nine when I woke up and crawled out of my tent, trying not to notice the cold that made my body feel brittle at 44 degrees below zero. I looked around carefully for polar bears. I could see none. But the twenty-mile-per-hour gusts of wind that whistled over the ice every ten or fifteen minutes were strong enough to kick the thin layer of fine snow into the air, cutting visibility to just a few yards. Between gusts there were lulls when the snow lay quiet. The wind still swept in from the north and the skies were clear, but I wondered if these strong gusts were the forerunners of a change.

Charlie stood up as I approached. His back had been to the wind and was crusted with a thin layer of snow. He was rested and ready for breakfast. I marveled again at his willingness to lie out on the ice without shelter from the bitter wind. He just curled up, back to the wind, and made the best of it. In the high Arctic desert there isn't even enough snow to cover the dogs and provide insulation. Their meager diet of frozen seal and ice somehow allows them to survive, although many die young. Through many generations of this lifestyle, the dogs of the Arctic have become strong and durable. They are survivors in the best sense of the word.

It was late and I was irritated at myself for having slept so long. The blisters on two fingers of my right hand had broken, leaving the flesh from the tips down to the second joints red, raw, and oozing a fluid tinged with blood. I taped them, but the pressure was too painful, so I bandaged them with gauze, which was only a slight improvement. The pain was wretched as I pulled my liner gloves on. My fingers were swollen and the tight fit moved the gauze, causing excruciating pain. I would just have to make do until they healed.

After a quick breakfast I carefully packed, making sure nothing blew away in the wind. In a cold climate even the simplest jobs take a long time, and when the wind blows it takes even longer. Everything has to be well anchored or it will never be seen again. My sore fingers slowed me, but I was finally ready just before noon for my latest start yet.

The ice ahead was a smooth highway covered with a thin layer of snow and a few hard-packed snowdrifts scattered about. The coast, four hundred yards to my left, was a flat icy plain extending far inland just as it had at Rapid Point. It was indented with narrow frozen bays but otherwise quite featureless. The sky, almost white from the reflecting ice beneath, stretched endlessly overhead to touch the horizons in all directions. It was like traveling in an enormous white bowl.

This part of Bathurst Island is known as Scoresby Hills, named for William Scoresby, a prominent whaling captain in the early nineteenth century who, in 1820, wrote *Account of the Arctic Regions*. But "hills" really stretched the imagination here on the coast, although farther inland, well beyond my sight, there were, according to my map, a few hills of five hundred to seven hundred feet elevation. As I turned into the wind with Charlie at my side, I felt dispirited. My hands were a mess, the wind soon froze my face mask, I still had around three hundred miles to go, and I was starting my day at the unheard-of hour of noon. I was grumpy and impatient.

A few minutes after we began, Charlie stepped over the right-hand rope leading to the sled, tangling his leash with the rope. It had happened before, but it had been no problem. We had always untangled in a couple of minutes. But this time I lost my temper and shouted at him, "Stupid dog, use your brains and stop getting tangled up." His reaction was immediate. He cringed, lay down on the ice, and dropped his head onto his paws, looking up at me with sad eyes.

My angry voice, which sounded louder in the silence, and the sight of a cringing Charlie jerked me to my senses. How could I shout at him like that? I felt ashamed. He had become a loving, faithful friend and had even saved my life yesterday. It was time to make up. "I'm so sorry, Charlie," I said as I bent down to pat him. The effect was electrifying. He jumped up and licked my gloved hand, waving his tail like a flag of victory. I hugged him and told him how much I loved him. He didn't have to tell me he loved me. I could see it. I resolved right then and there that, no matter what happened, I wouldn't speak to Charlie like that again. I skied off in a much better frame of mind with a happy Charlie at my side. No more grumpiness. Charlie was watching.

According to my map, Baring Island to the east was about twenty-five miles away, too far for me to see from sea level across the carpet of ice that stretched to touch its shores. My constant companion, the Bathurst Island coastline, still beckoned to the west. My map showed the next fifteen miles ahead to be an extension of the same wide coastal plain I could see to my left, with little to distinguish the land ice from the floating sea ice. A desolate expanse.

The smooth ice provided the fastest skiing of the trip so far. Perhaps I could make up for my late start. The wind stopped gusting and settled down to a steady fifteen miles per hour. At 44 below zero, the wind chill was about 90 degrees below zero. Because I was heading into the wind a crust of ice soon covered my mask and crept down my jacket front. After an hour Charlie's face was also covered with a thin coating of ice. It would have been a relief to have the wind behind us, but I didn't dare think such thoughts. A south wind would only bring stormy weather. As I skied on, I still kept up my routine of stopping every ten minutes or so to check behind us for bears. I still had a horror of a bear sneaking up behind. But I saw no bears. In fact, I hadn't seen a track since just south of Rapid Point.

It was three o'clock before I stopped for a drink. Charlie and I settled down behind my sled out of the wind. I took my mask off and saw that it was coated with a thick layer of ice. After a few walnuts, crackers, and a warm drink I tried to put it on again. It was a frozen board. I chopped at the ice with my axe, then broke the rest off. Even so I was glad to put it back on. At least it kept the wind from freezing my face and nose. Now I regretted that I had brought only one mask with me. At least two would have allowed me to alternate, instead of struggling with only one that was always wet or frozen. But I reasoned that one cold, frozen mask was better than none at all. Anytime I was tempted to leave it off, I had only to remember the faces I had seen with the ends of noses lost to frostbite because the owner of the nose refused to wear a mask. Ice coated Charlie's face. I brushed some of it off, then stopped. Perhaps it would act as a mask and help protect him from the wind. I couldn't see more than a half mile ahead now. The wind was blowing the snow twenty feet into the air, almost hiding the coastline. I replaced my goggles with sunglasses thinking I might have better visibility, but they froze my skin wherever the cold plastic touched, so I quickly changed back to my goggles. So much for that idea.

We had traveled about six miles when Charlie hit on a bright idea of his own. He discovered that if he leaned lightly on my right leg, he would get an automatic side scratch as I skied back and forth. At first I thought, "How cute," but soon changed my mind when he leaned too hard and his ninety-three pounds pushed me over in a tangled heap on the ice. At that moment I was glad we were alone, thankful that no one could see me now. This was definitely undignified, lying in a tangled pile of legs, skis, and sled rope, with a big, black dog staring quizzically at my face.

I untangled myself, pointed us north again, and set

out once more. It was obvious by now that this expedition might be many things, but it was not boring. Charlie and the polar bears saw to that. He began leaning on me again so I invented a new ski technique, jerking my right knee out to the side to signal Charlie when he was leaning too hard. We developed a nice but unorthodox rhythm. Still, I hoped a bump rather than a scratch would discourage Charlie's little game.

At eight miles my map showed a sandbar three quarters of a mile offshore from Bathurst Island. But the only sign I could see of it was a two- or three-foot rise of broken ice, as if something was trying to push through to the surface. Currents were swirling around the sandbar roughing up the ice and I could hear it murmuring quietly. It was a tired, sad sound, as if the ice longed for peace that never came from the swift currents below.

There was another sandbar just ahead, to my left, jutting out from the shore, making the ice even rougher. I skied between the two bars and stopped to camp on the north side, clear of the rough, noisy ice. We had traveled ten miles—respectable for such a late start. It was six o'clock, the wind was gusting over twenty miles per hour, and visibility was no more than two hundred yards. I could hardly see the coast at all through the blowing snow. The stronger gusts raced by with a loud whistle, dying away into the distance.

I staked Charlie out only six feet from the tent, hoping he would get some shelter from the wind and still be able to see or hear a bear in time to warn me. It was torture putting my tent up. My hands were in bad shape. More blisters had burst during the day as I skied, but I chose not to look at them until I had finished all my camp jobs. I was afraid that if I did, my hands might begin to feel as bad as they looked.

It was even worse putting the radio antenna up. It was important to align the antenna with base camp to the south. If it pointed east or west, the signal was too weak to reach the camp. That night after several tries I was unable to get through so I must not have aligned the antenna correctly. After I was greeted by silence several times, I sent the message, "Kiwi expedition transmitting in the blind." It was the traditional invitation to anyone listening to answer. My signal was picked up by Peter, the manager of a tourist camp at Eureka, three hundred miles away to the northeast. He relayed my position to base camp at Resolute.

Lighting the stove felt like one long scream. But I had to at least melt ice for water. I knew I had to eat and drink to survive, but I didn't eat much. By the time I had lit the stove, I was cold and the whole exercise of cooking dinner was rapidly becoming too much trouble. It was such slow work. I succumbed to the temptation to just make do, although in the back of my mind common sense lurked, telling me that I was wrong to take shortcuts with eating and drinking. But just then it seemed more convenient to listen to common sense tomorrow, so I ate only a small bowl of rice and drank two cups of hot chocolate.

After my sparse dinner I peeled off my inner gloves. The sight made me sick to my stomach. All the blisters had broken, leaving nine fingers raw from the tips down to the second joints, oozing the same blood-tinged fluid. My left little finger was the only one I had to remind me of what a healthy finger should look like. I bathed the rest in warm water left over from dinner, dressed them lightly with gauze, and slid my hands into a large pair of fluffy pile mitts to protect them. Then I sat there in my tent feeling sorry for myself. What a mess. After my skimpy dinner I was still hungry and thirsty, I was cold and my hands had become a serious problem.

I knew self-pitying thoughts would never get me to the pole. I had to replace the negatives with positives as soon as possible, and as I began to think about my situation, I could see several positives already. First of all, my hands were only temporarily damaged. After all, the flesh on my fingers was alive. Dead fingers would turn black. Mine were a mixture of red and pink, and even the pain proved that there was abundant life in each one. I had lots of food and fuel with me. In fact I had planned my food supply to last forty days in case of an emergency. I had already come to grips with the problems of coexisting with polar bears, and although I had never been more scared in my whole life, I had managed successfully to confront each bear as it came along.

With such thoughts, all at once the self-pity left me and I felt hopeful and confident again. This was a journey of credits and debits. Every time I dipped into the debit column, I had to pull myself over into the credit side without delay.

I always wore gloves when I slept, not only to keep my hands warm, but also to be prepared in case I had to dash from the tent to greet a polar bear. I wore my camp booties to bed for the same reasons. This was no place for stocking feet in an emergency. To make sure I was even more ready for a fast exit, I never pulled the zipper all the way up on the sleeping bag, and the zipper on the tent door had an extra-long pull tab so I could grab it without looking for it. My flare gun stayed alongside my sleeping bag. But I always laid the rifle down with the butt just outside the door within easy reach. I couldn't keep it in the tent because any warmth caused condensation around the firing mechanism, which would quickly freeze outside the tent, making the rifle useless. My big worry at night was whether I could get out of the tent in time to greet a bear. I had no plans to entertain a bear inside.

It was nine o'clock and the wind, although still strong, seemed to be tearing at the tent walls a little less now. I peeked out the door at Charlie. He was curled up, apparently asleep, getting some shelter from his sled and a little from the tent. I hated to leave him out there, but he was my best bet if a polar bear came close. It was still difficult to push away my guilty thoughts about leaving Charlie outside, but I finally fell asleep to the rhythmic flapping of the tent.

I woke at two, listening for the wind. It had died down and everything was still. I looked out of the tent and it was light again. When I began this journey a gray dusk settled over us about eight o'clock at night. Now a gray light lasted only about six hours from around 9:00 P.M. to about 3:00 A.M. Soon there would be twenty-four hours of daylight. I checked on Charlie. He looked peaceful and I soon fell asleep again.

DAY 7

It was cold and sunny as I climbed out of my tent to start another day. Seven straight days of clear skies was more than I had expected. It was surprising, given the changeable nature of Arctic weather. But I wasn't complaining. The golden rays of early morning sun were pushing their way through a thin fog of ice crystals. There was just a hint of a halo around the sun. I felt a little uneasy. Did these subtle signs mean a change from the stable weather pattern of the last six days? I hoped not.

Charlie was already up. As I approached him, as usual

he flopped down on the ice on his back, white paws in the air, waiting for me to scratch his tummy. This did not strike me as the proper pose for a ferocious polar bear guard dog. He looked like a big affectionate house pet with nothing better to do than make himself lovable. I knelt and scratched the white blaze that ran all the way along his tummy and up his chest, using my knuckles because my fingertips were too sore. I dug my knuckles in hard. He loved it. He closed his eyes and floated temporarily off to doggy heaven.

I was hungry, so I ate most of two bowls of granola and shared part of the second one with Charlie, much to his delight. Then it was time to pack up and leave for another day's travel. As always the plan was to cover as many miles as possible. I had long ago decided that my best defense against polar bears was to reach the pole and then go home. But first of all we had to reach the pole.

Home and family seemed to be farther away each day. I was too busy surviving to be really homesick, but I often thought of everyone I had left behind and looked forward to seeing them again. Knowing Bill and my family, I was becoming more and more concerned about the worry I must be causing them. Because that weighed more heavily on my conscience every day, I decided to be very careful about what I told base camp on the radio at night. They would still worry, but they could hear the whole story when I was safely back home.

Starting out that day, I saw that the coastline was still flat, with few distinguishing features. My map showed the Moses Robinson River mouth to be about six miles ahead. At least that was something to aim for. I found that if I divided my journey into segments, each day's travel went faster. The ice crystal fog was increasing in density. I had to squint as I strained to see the coastline only a half mile away. But at least I didn't have to deal with the wind.

As the ice fog grew even denser, reflected sunlight created a pale golden curtain around us that seemed to be made of the finest, softest chiffon. Without thinking, I put my hand out to touch it but met only empty space. I was standing in a golden world alone with Charlie, a soft, gentle world, and I wished everyone could see it and know the feeling of tranquility that went with it. The phenomenon of sunlight and ice crystals had turned this harsh, unforgiving polar desert into an oasis of quiet, golden beauty. Skiing slowly, I wished I could make the scene last forever.

The terrain ahead of me was covered with large patches of hard-packed snow, some fifty yards across, interrupted with ridges of driven snow as high as two feet. The hard-packed snow between the ridges gave plenty of grip to my skis. In the Arctic, the wind packs the fine, white grains of the sparse snowfall into a thick, solid crust, and Charlie and I pulled our sleds with ease.

The coastline had almost disappeared in the thick fog. So instead of using that for a direction guide, I made a mental note of where my shadow was pointing. My watch read 8:30 A.M. and I was traveling due north. The sun was now in the east and swinging south. My shadow was pointing northwest and would change its angle fifteen degrees every hour. As long as the sun could penetrate the thick fog, I would follow the direction of my shadow.

The temperature seemed to be rising. This, coupled with the fog curtain and the halo around the sun, convinced me that there soon would be weather changes for the worse. I increased my speed so that if a storm was approaching I would travel at least a reasonable number of miles that day. There was still no wind, just an eerie calm. And by 9:30 the golden curtain around us had faded to a white, dense fog. The early morning magic had disappeared as if it had never been there. I was still navigating by my shadow, which now showed only as a gray patch on the snow and ice. I knew that Bathurst Island was somewhere in the fog to the west, but for me right now, it didn't exist.

It was difficult to watch for bears. I hoped their creamy white coats would show up in the surrounding white. But as always Charlie would be my best warning. I kept a close eye on his reactions rather than staring through the ice fog trying to see a bear that I hoped wasn't there. We were traveling in a world only a few yards wide. I tried not to dwell on what might be beyond those few yards.

I was also having a problem with depth perception. Conditions weren't a complete white-out, but were bad enough so that I had to travel at a slower pace to see the hollows and ridges of the ice pack. Sometimes I skied straight into a shallow ridge and stumbled before I saw it; at other times I dropped unexpectedly into a hollow. I was constantly catching my balance, unable to flow with a distance-consuming stride.

There was still enough sun shining through the fog to cast a shadow and create some depth perception. In a true white-out, light coming from all directions has the same strength and casts no shadows. The horizon disappears and space, even close by, has no depth. It is impossible to know where the surface is, and anyone traveling on foot in such conditions stumbles about as if the world has dropped away. I wondered aloud to Charlie how polar bears deal with these conditions. He wasn't having any problems. Sometimes a stumble would send me colliding into him, but he accepted it all with his usual dignity. But surely he must have wondered at my sudden inability to keep to my side of the road.

At about 1:00 P.M. the fog began to thin and suddenly I stopped. There appeared to be a smooth, rounded cliff about twenty feet high only ten feet in front of me and curving around to my left. I couldn't imagine where it came from. I looked at my map trying to figure where I had gone wrong. It showed a flat coastline with a few minor river mouths scattered along the shore edge. The terrain around us was uneven, with rough-edged slabs and chunks of ice jutting into the air, and narrow cracks in the ice zigzagging through the maze. At first I thought I must have turned west and not realized I had crossed the Bathurst coastline in the fog. Had I stumbled in the wrong direction until I finally reached an inland cliff? It didn't make sense. I had complete confidence in navigating using only the sun and my shadow.

Then I looked carefully around me. The numerous cracks and chunks of broken ice told me that I was still on the ice pack. When I listened I could even hear a faint grating sound drifting up from the floating ice beneath my feet. But where could this cliff have come from? Perhaps it was an island not on the map. I stood there trying to solve the puzzle when all at once the fog lifted and my "cliff" disappeared as though by magic. In its place I saw a low, icy coastal plain about a quarter of a mile in front of me curving back to my left. The ice pack around me was rough and disturbed by a now frozen river.

I was dumbfounded. I had been fooled by the lack of depth perception. There was no contrast or scale to measure height and distance on this foggy day in a completely white world. It's a familiar phenomenon in the Arctic. There are many humorous stories of Arctic hunters stalking a large animal in the distance only to find that it has turned into a small Arctic fox or hare just a few feet away. Vilhjalmur Stefansson wrote about such experiences in *My Life with the Eskimo,* and history books tell us of "islands" and great "cliffs" being mapped by early explorers who suddenly found their discoveries were nothing more than large protruding pieces of ice.

I was relieved to find that my "cliff" had disappeared. The fog wavered back and forth, gradually thinning and increasing visibility. Now I could see where to put my skis and was able to tell where I was. I had traveled north up the coast to where the land curves eastward, forming a bay. In the fog I had traveled straight toward the bay. My guess was that I must be close to the coastal outlet of the Moses Robinson River. I swung northeast, following the curve of the land, and sure enough in a half hour I saw a large, frozen river mouth. The Moses Robinson originated from a plateau far inland at an elevation of around seven hundred feet and emptied into the sea over a wide area of land jutting out from the coast almost no higher than the sea ice. The river was frozen in winter and spring, but during the later summer months I could imagine the river water flowing off the plateau and churning the sea ice into a broken mass.

The day's puzzle had been solved, but I still had to cover more miles. I increased my speed and headed up the coast as the fog disappeared. I welcomed the improved visibility. In another half hour the ice smoothed out and I made good time for the next five miles. At about three miles the coastal land had become steeper.

A one-hundred-foot cliff ran along the edge of the icy beach for a mile and a half, a contrast to the flat land I had passed for the last several miles. Then it flattened again to a coastal plain that extended to a place called Airstrip Point. I could only imagine how this place got its name. Perhaps some thankful pilot found a flat landing spot when he needed it most.

It was 6:00 P.M. so I decided to camp about half a mile before the point. Charlie and I had traveled eleven miles in spite of the fog and the stretch of rough ice. But as I made camp I became increasingly concerned about the weather. It had warmed to 31 degrees below zero, a ten-degree increase since seven that morning, and it showed no signs of cooling off as it normally did in the evening. A light north wind whispered by the tent, barely moving the fabric. The fog was gone and I could see clearly in all directions. Were these harbingers of a storm from the south? Because I felt so uneasy about the weather, I tied the tent down with two extra ice screws just in case the wind picked up.

I tried to ignore my hands as I cooked dinner. Attaching the fuel line to the stove had been painful but after some careful maneuvering I pushed the line into the stove's small fuel hole. I had Charlie as a companion. He hadn't lain down to sleep as soon as he finished his dog food. Instead he fussed and cried until I brought him to the tent door, close to where I was cooking dinner inside. He didn't fool me one bit. I could see he wanted to share my dinner. He lay down in the tent doorway attached by his chain to an ice screw. With his head on his paws he watched every move I made. When I added hot water to my bowl of rice and raised a spoonful to my lips, Charlie immediately stood up, begging. Here we go again, I thought, that begging look. I suc-

cumbed and put two spoonfuls of rice on the ice in front
of him. It was gone in a flash so I turned my back,
hoping to finish my meal in peace, but halfway through
my eyes turned in Charlie's direction as if pulled by a
magnet. He had reached toward me as far as his chain
would allow and I met two brown eyes an inch away
from mine. The message in those eyes was clear.
"Won't you share just a little more?"

It was, of course, impossible to refuse so I gave him
half of what was left, followed by a handful of crackers
and a little milk powder. When it was time for him to
leave for his usual spot, I had to pull him away as he
looked back over his shoulder at the tent. It was very
clear that his next goal was to persuade me to let him
inside the tent. I resolved to be very firm and maintain
strict discipline because I knew that the best place for
Charlie to bear-watch was about twenty feet away from
the tent. But I also knew this was going to be a real test.
Charlie's powers of persuasion were considerable and
quite possibly greater than my powers of discipline.

I radioed base camp at the usual hour and anxiously
asked for a weather forecast. Terry told me there was a
possibility of a storm in the next day or two.

The temperature was steady at 31 below, the wind
still only a whisper, and after a final good night hug for
Charlie and one last look around for bears, I crawled
into my tent. I wore heavy insulated ski boots, which
were a struggle to pull off at the best of times. Now it
was almost impossible with hands that looked more like
bloody clubs. But the boots had to come off. If I climbed
into my sleeping bag with them on, my feet would
freeze. It took me about fifteen minutes to pull them off
and I didn't look forward to the struggle to put them
back on, but I decided to worry about that in the morn-

ing. My hands could also wait until morning. I took off my warm, windproof outer mitts, leaving the liner gloves on, and I climbed into my sleeping bag. I lay watching the gentle, swaying movement of the tent side-walls as the light breeze drifted by. The ice was silent. It was easy to fall asleep.

DAY 8

The south wind I dreaded had arrived. Sometime during the night while I slept the wind had changed direction, and I stood outside the tent looking for signs of the storm I knew a south wind could bring. The weather looked good, but I decided on an early start just in case. I fed Charlie, broke camp, and loaded my sled as fast as I could. Noting that the ropes around the dog food bags on Charlie's sled had worked loose during yesterday's travel, I retied them carefully. Putting my boots back on was my last job. Again it was a painful struggle as I tried not to use my fingers. My only con-solation was that the job would become easier as my hands improved.

We left at 7:00 A.M., and even though a south wind could bring a storm, the wind at my back felt good. Up to now it had blown straight into our faces. Charlie didn't complain when we traveled into the wind, but I did. My mask always turned into a frozen lump, my eyelashes froze, and worse still, I had to be careful that my eyes didn't freeze when I couldn't wear my goggles because of fogging. I tried to wear goggles as often as possible, but when fog froze on the lenses, I had to take them off to watch for bears, which left my eyes unpro-tected from the wind. The hood on my parka kept blowing off in a strong head wind and I was constantly grabbing it to pull it back on. But now the south wind at our backs solved those problems.

We turned slightly east to go around Airstrip Point. The ice there was jumbled. In summertime a minor un-named river flowed over the low, barren land of the point to meet the sea. Now it was frozen and the land was hidden under a thick blanket of ice as we passed by.

At the point we turned north again. Ahead I could see high coastal cliffs stretching into the distance. In places they rose two hundred feet almost straight up out of the ice-covered sea. A thick layer of ice also covered the clifftops like glistening white frosting on a cake, and their sides were streaked with long tongues of blue-white ice that reached down to the sea ice below. Each ledge, large and small, held an icy frosting while the exposed rock was a pale sandy color. The jagged cliffs were a dramatic contrast to the flat lowlands we had left behind us. I could see no sign of any bird life on the cliffs. It was still too early and too icy cold. The cliffs stood silent and barren.

The wind was increasing. The thin layer of snow, instead of blowing toward us as it had done for seven days, now blew along the surface of the ice in front of us in long fingers silently pointing north, leading the way. At ten o'clock we were a half mile off the coast, dwarfed by the towering cliffs. I stopped to eat a few crackers and drink some warm liquid from my thermos. It was a good time to rearrange my sled load. In my haste to leave camp that morning, and favoring my sore fingers, I must have put too much weight on one side. Now the load was leaning so much it practically shouted at me to do something to right it. I grumbled at myself for not having been more careful. Much easier and faster to pack in camp than on the journey in an unfriendly wind.

By the time I had taken off the tie-down ropes and repacked the entire load, the wind had increased enough to pick the snow off the surface of the ice and swirl it around the sled. The fine snow blew high into the air, cutting visibility in half. Earlier that morning as we rounded Airstrip Point, I had seen the faint outline of Des Voeux Island eight miles to the east. Now the island had disappeared behind a wall of blowing snow.

I anxiously looked back at the approaching storm. A dark gray bank of clouds and blowing snow stretched as far to the east as I could see and engulfed Bathurst to the west. It was still several miles to the south, but it would soon catch up with us.

I fed Charlie some crackers and grabbed more for myself before skiing on. I couldn't tell how fast the storm was traveling. Perhaps I could cover a few more miles before it engulfed us. I felt vulnerable out there alone, being chased down by a storm. If the bank of clouds behind us was being driven by high winds, I would have to be careful to stop in time to put up my tent. In a strong wind my tent could soon become a sail that I knew I couldn't handle alone.

The wind speed gradually picked up. Although the temperature was higher than yesterday, the cold wind was penetrating. I wore a sherpa type hat with earflaps and a strap that tied under my chin. Every day of my journey the strap had frozen, turning it into a sharp cord across my throat. Today was too much. It had become so thickly encrusted with ice that it was actually beginning to cut my skin when I turned my head. I stopped and severed the frozen straps with my pocket knife. That fixed the problem in an instant.

I looked ahead through the blowing snow and could

see a peak standing above the coastal cliffs. It was Cocks-
comb Peak, 363 feet in elevation, the highest point we
had passed on the journey so far. My climbing instincts
aroused, I wondered what the summit was like. It appeared wide and rounded. It looked like an easy climb.
The northern slope plunged steeply down to the flat,
ice-covered plain of Sargent Point ahead of us.

I stopped to measure the wind speed and temperature. The readings were twelve to fifteen miles per hour
and minus 22 degrees. The storm was pushing warmer
air ahead of it. It was only 1:00 P.M. and the storm still
hadn't caught us so I kept going, hoping to at least reach
Sargent Point. Perhaps I could find shelter from the approaching storm in a bay on the northern side of the
point.

The blowing snow slowed travel. I couldn't see the
lumps of ice that were waiting to trip my skis. Visibility
worsened, then depth perception played tricks on me. I
tried to step over a lump of ice only to find it to be
several feet ahead of me. Everything took on a gray,
bleak look.

Finally Sargent Point appeared through the billowing
snow. As I stumbled over the lumps and sharp edges of
ice, I could see a flat plain that belonged to another
world, gray and far away. The lack of depth perception
made everything seem unreal. The storm had caught up
to us, enveloping us in a gray mist of blowing snow in
which the only sound was the wind, and all I could see
were uneven shapes of ice and the low coastline that
seemed very far away. Distance had no meaning. Was
the coastline four feet or four hundred feet away? I
stopped and looked around. I felt uneasy, as if I was the
only person in a rapidly shrinking gray world. My surroundings took on a mystical quality and fear began to
creep slowly into my mind. I skied a few more yards,

trying to adjust to the new conditions and regain a sense of reality. I touched Charlie on his broad back. At least he was real, and gradually I regained my own sense of reality and pushed the fear away. I tried to control the fear by keeping a tight grasp on reality, concentrating on things such as ski technique and navigation, constantly working to travel faster.

But there is really no way to prepare yourself for the emotions of being alone in the great polar desert. There is nothing familiar to pin emotions on. It is a white world devoid of the wide spectrum of colors, noises, and familiar objects of civilization. When this unfamiliar, lonely world is reduced to a small gray patch by a storm in which distance sometimes has no meaning and familiar objects do not exist, it can be traumatic. Alone in an enormous expanse where humans are not meant to live, in constant fear of attack by polar bears, I could never really relax. I always had to maintain strict control over my thoughts and emotions. My survival depended on it.

The wind hadn't increased, but visibility and depth perception were virtually nonexistent. I was stumbling over unseen lumps of ice and my progress was slow. It was time to make camp. Charlie didn't seem to care one way or the other. He was encrusted with snow, but he was at home in this weather and didn't seem the least perturbed. His calm confidence was good for me.

I was standing facing north, releasing the buckle on my sled harness, when I saw a small animal stepping off the shoreline onto the sea ice. I strained through the gray gloom trying to figure out what kind of animal it was. I looked at Charlie. He was watching with concentrated interest but not much concern. It had to be an Arctic fox, I thought, but where was its long bushy tail? It had none. Then suddenly it dawned on me. Of course, it was a tiny bear cub. I quickly looked around for its mother, but there was no sign of her. Perhaps she was dead. My mind was a whirl. There was no way I could leave such a small helpless cub out there all alone. I said to Charlie, "How in the world am I going to catch it, and when I do, how will I keep it on my sled until I can radio the wildlife people to come and rescue it?" I couldn't take it to the pole with me. What would I feed it? I saw it walk out onto the ice, then stand up to look at us. I took that as a good sign. At least it wasn't frightened of us. Charlie wasn't making a sound. That was a good sign too.

I felt sorry for the tiny cub. I dropped my harness, took my skis off, and tied Charlie to the sled so he wouldn't get in the way. A plan was developing. If I approached slowly the cub might come to me. After all, it was surely too small to want to do anything but find its mother.

The light was gray and the air was filled with blowing snow as I walked perhaps twenty steps with my hand outstretched in a most inviting manner. The cub moved several quick paces to the right just as the wind and swirling snow eased slightly. Before my eyes, in the changing deceptive light, the tiny cub suddenly became a full-grown polar bear, and there I was without a weapon to defend myself, trying to catch it to put on my sled and keep it safe. I froze with shock. I couldn't turn and run for my flare gun. That would invite the bear to chase me and I would surely lose the race. I wasn't even sure how far away it was because of the visibility and depth perception problem, but I guessed about one hundred feet.

With my heart thumping, I slowly inched backward, a half step at a time, keeping my eyes fixed on the bear.

Finally, after what seemed an eternity, I felt my flare gun and rifle behind me on my sled. I carefully drew them to the front of the sled and stood waiting to see what the bear's next move would be. Charlie was stretched to the end of his chain, staring intently at the bear, quietly growling. The bear stopped moving to our right and turned to face us. He stood looking at us for several minutes, then moved to the right and stopped again to look at us. Then he took two or three paces toward us but stopped when Charlie's growling increased in volume. Finally the bear turned and walked off to the north without another look, vanishing in the gray gloom that engulfed us.

I stood there long after the bear had left. I couldn't believe what I had just tried to do. How absurd. Catch a thousand-pound polar bear and put it on my sled? This was a story I certainly wouldn't tell anyone. They would think I was crazy. Then I wondered what that bear had thought when a strange two-legged creature began walking toward him with an outstretched hand. I was probably the first human he had ever seen and perhaps he walked away shaking his head in puzzlement. As for me, I had learned a valuable lesson. On this journey all animals would be full-grown polar bears until proven otherwise!

I'm not sure if Charlie had been deceived by the lack of depth perception, as I was. I'm sure he knew it was a bear from the outset. He also probably sensed that it was more curious than aggressive. By this time I was certain he instinctively knew the difference in the moods of polar bears.

It was three o'clock now and the storm had grown no worse. The south wind had stabilized at about fifteen miles per hour and the temperature had risen rapidly to minus 19 degrees. I made camp and fed Charlie after staking him out about twenty feet in front of the tent. Uncertain how long the storm would last, I chopped several chunks of ice to melt for water and laid them at the tent door within easy reach. It wouldn't be much fun trying to chop ice if the wind became stronger. I looked forward to the shelter of the tent. The wind-driven snow was seeping into my clothing like fine sand. Even as I put up my tent and unloaded my sled, the snow was into everything, even my sleeping bag.

I checked Charlie. He was well sheltered with his sled on the south side for protection. Just before ducking into my tent, I went through the usual ritual of a last look-around for bears. I saw something moving to the south. Again, it was hard to tell just how far away it was. I mentally tried to push the gray blanket of blowing snow aside to see more clearly through the dim light. At first I thought it was two snowmobiles side by side. I had been told in my nightly radio call two days ago that an Australian snowmobile expedition had left Resolute Bay for the magnetic North Pole. They expected to pass me in the next day or so. But it was too soon for them to be here, especially considering the unexpectedly rough ice I had encountered, which would slow them down. Mindful of my recent lesson, I suspected a polar bear, and standing beside a watchful Charlie, I had my rifle and flare gun ready.

Then through the grayness I saw the bear. He was coming straight at us with that peculiar pigeon-toed gait that made him appear to be two moving objects side by side in this gloomy light. At 150 feet I fired two warning shots from my rifle, then began shooting flares in front of him as fast as I could load and pull the trigger. He did not stop. He kept coming at us with a determined gait that meant business. Traveling north, he wasn't going around us or the tent. The warning shots and flares so far meant nothing to him. He was a big-boned animal but looked thinner than the others I had so far encountered, and that could mean a hungry bear who thought he had discovered an easy meal.

When he was about seventy-five feet away things looked serious. He was walking in a straight line right at us and nothing was turning him away. I was desperate. I had to make something work and right now. A couple more fast flares, then it would be up to Charlie. The next flare I fired landed almost on the bear's front left foot, too close for his comfort. He jumped and veered to his right. The next one landed right under his nose, making him jump backward. Charlie charged with a vicious, snarling leap to the end of his chain, trying to get at the bear. I kept up the barrage of flares, landing them on the ice close to the bear's front feet. My aim had improved and I was laying them where I wanted them to go. It worked. Under a deluge of burning red flares at his feet, the bear backed away to the east in a wide circle. He was heading again almost in a northerly direction when he stopped as if reluctant to give up. I fired four more flares close to his feet. That was too much. He left without his dinner.

Charlie was straining at his chain and frothing at the mouth. His bark sounded almost hoarse. My hand shook so much as I laid the flare gun down that I nearly dropped it. That had been a close call and I was reminded again of how dangerous polar bears are. Trying to regain control of my emotions, wondering again if it would be possible to survive this journey, I stood watching in the cold wind for another fifteen minutes in case the bear returned. A thin, hungry bear might not give up easily. He could sneak close in this weather without being seen. But Charlie had quieted down. He seemed satisfied that the bear had left. I knelt on the cold hard ice and patted him. If I had let him go, he would still be out there with the bear. I was glad it hadn't come to that.

I checked on Charlie's shelter and walked to my tent. I was shivering in the bleak cold and wanted to get out of the wind that had increased in strength and stung my face and eyes with snow.

Just as I was about to go into the tent I looked back at Charlie. He hadn't curled up on the ice yet. Instead he was watching me, and his look said, "What about me out in this cold?" Common sense told me that Arctic dogs live outside on the ice with no shelter in far worse weather than this all their lives. But then I thought this is not only an Arctic dog, he's Charlie. Perhaps, just once, he can sleep in the sheltered porch area at the front of the tent. Tomorrow he can sleep in his usual place outside.

I walked back to him, unsnapping his chain, and said, "Okay, Charlie, tonight you can sleep in the porch as a special treat." But before the words were out of my mouth, he made a beeline for the tent. Not even pausing at the porch, he leaped into my sleeping bag, which was already laid out for my cold, shivering body to slip into. I ran after him. "No, Charlie, that's my place," I said sternly. "You take the porch." But in an instant he was curled up in the sleeping bag, ready for sleep.

There was no way I would put up with that. "Charlie, get out of there," I said. His only response was to tuck his nose farther into his curled-up tail. I pulled on his collar. No response. "I'll push you out," I threatened. I knelt beside him and pushed. Nothing moved. I kept pushing, trying to roll him out. How was I going to get this ninety-three-pound canine that had turned into a limp noodle out of my sleeping bag?

I already knew the answer. I might as well give up and make do. I was so cold that as I pulled off my boots and took off my outer jacket I hardly noticed my hands. "Charlie, this is not going to work," I said as I eased into the space alongside him. "When I warm up you have to go."

I wasn't comfortable, but at least I got some much-needed warmth into my body and a half hour later I was no longer shivering. I began to plan different tactics to get rid of Charlie. I climbed out of the bag and prepared a comfortable clear area in the porch for him. Then I sat down with my feet in the sleeping bag and slid them underneath his body. He immediately opened his eyes. He didn't like the two lumps wiggling under him, but I kept it up until with a great sigh he sat up. As quick as lightning, I slid into his space and spread out, taking up all the bag area I could. That did it. He gave up and moved out. Victory was mine. I got up and led him by his collar to his new accommodations in the porch. He flopped down in a ball and went to sleep. At least he had tried.

I cooked dinner, then radioed base camp. It was already eight o'clock. The temperature had risen even more, to only minus 8 degrees Fahrenheit, but the wind had increased to a strong twenty-seven miles per hour. I was anxious to hear a weather forecast. It wasn't good. "Expect more strong winds from the south," Terry said, then told me that the snowmobile expedition had turned back when the storm struck them about fifty miles behind me. There were four snowmobiles and two of them had lost their way in the storm. I could understand why. The awful visibility made traveling dangerous.

I was worried at the thought of anyone lost out there on the rough ice in the worsening storm, but at least one problem had been solved. The snowmobile expedition had planned to rendezvous with me and I was concerned that my goal of a strictly solo expedition would be compromised by such a meeting. One reason for my expedition was to learn to exist alone in this vast polar desert. Others had traveled in groups or pairs, which is a vastly different experience from a solo journey without encounters with fellow humans. It was a chance of a lifetime for me to experience a truly solo journey on foot to the pole. Now, as I was the only expedition going to the magnetic North Pole this year, I would be able to realize my goal. However, I was unhappy at the thought of anyone lost in a storm like the one raging outside my tent. As I signed off the radio conversation, Terry promised to have more news tomorrow night. I prayed it would be good news for the snowmobile expedition.

To make sure my little "house" would stay in one place that night, I put my jacket on and went outside to check that the tie-down lines were tight and all was ready to wait out the storm. The wind took my breath away as I faced into it. Leaning to stay upright, I tightened two ice screws and tied an extra rope to my sled so that it couldn't break free. In no time my clothes were caked with driven snow, even under my jacket. When I climbed into the tent I was cold again. And I was still worried about bears. The wind was sweeping across the ice and slamming into the tent. The noise of the wind and the flapping tent were too loud for me to hear a bear. It was the first storm of our journey and I wondered if Charlie could sense a bear in this awful racket.

I dusted the snow off my clothes as best I could and sat upright in my sleeping bag listening for bears. But it was so cold that I decided to take my chances. Maybe the bears would stay away in this storm. It was time for sleep. Crawling into my bag, I hoped for good weather tomorrow and reached out to pat Charlie. Even if my discipline was slowly crumbling, it was nice to have him close.

DAY 9

I didn't need to look out to know the storm was still with us. I reached past a sleeping Charlie to where the thermometer was hanging from a tent tie-down rope outside the door. It was minus 20 degrees and I was surprised at how much the temperature had risen since yesterday morning. The wind sounded very uninviting but I needed to know if there was any chance at all of traveling today. I climbed out of my warm sleeping bag and struggled into my outer jacket. It was cold and stiff with ice. I hadn't deiced it last night over my stove. I had only wanted to crawl into my warm sleeping bag to escape the numbing cold.

Deicing had become a nightly job. After several hours of skiing during the day, a thick layer of ice formed on my mask, down the front of my jacket, and yesterday even around the collar, making it difficult to turn my head and almost impossible to unzip my jacket. I used my mountain-climbing ice axe to scrape the ice off the zipper when I took off my jacket. By the third day out I set aside time each night to melt the ice off my mask and jacket after I had eaten dinner and called base camp. Hunched over the stove each night thawing my clothes, at least I was able to take advantage of the extra warmth.

That morning I struggled into my still-frozen jacket, but the zipper wouldn't cooperate at all so I pulled on my hat and crawled out the door in my soft camp boots. Charlie was still curled up in the porch and I invited him to come outside with me, but after getting no response I went without him.

He was smart. When I stood up the wind caught me with its full force. My unzipped jacket was thrown open and the wind poured into my sweater and inner clothing. The icy blast of cold air on my chest went to the bone. Grabbing my jacket front, I clutched it to me, trying to keep the wind out. Unable to see through the swirling snow, I staggered around the tent trying to check on tie-down ropes, but it was impossible to keep my jacket closed. The driving snow was tearing at my unprotected eyes. Hunching over, I groped my way back and dived through the doorway into the tent, relieved to be out of the howling wind. It would be impossible to travel.

I took my snow-caked hat and jacket off and squirmed into my down parka. It was so large that it fitted around me like a small sleeping bag. I was deeply disappointed and frustrated that we couldn't leave. It didn't look too promising now, but perhaps we could travel in the afternoon. I decided to be ready to go as soon as the weather broke.

The first job was breakfast. Charlie didn't even look up when I put a large handful of dog food in front of him. He was still curled up into a tight black furry ball with his nose tucked out of sight. I was a little worried about him when he didn't respond at all. So I decided to experiment. I placed two peanut butter cups on his tail in front of where I thought his nose should be. As if by magic they both instantly disappeared into the depths of all that thick black fur. No need to worry. Charlie was fine. He was curled up to conserve body heat. As I watched him I thought about the other dogs I had seen at Resolute. They too curled up and simply waited out the storms. I checked Charlie's chain, slackening it a little so he could get up to stretch or go outside.

I lit the stove and melted ice for water. When the water was warm I mixed it up in a bowl of granola and milk powder and added a few peanut butter cups for a little variety. It tasted quite good, although I wouldn't recommend it as a gourmet delight.

I had been trying to ignore my hands for the past two days, reasoning that if I didn't acknowledge the pain they would feel better. But now with time to spare perhaps there was something I could do to help them. My fingers were a sorry sight. With the top layer of skin gone, they were raw and bleeding and cracks were forming on the tips. The cold, dry air and the fact that I had to use them all the time made them even worse. I was unable to give them a chance to heal. It made no difference to the pain if I bandaged them or not. But there was no infection at all so I concluded that no permanent harm would come to them. I kept at least one pair of liner gloves on most of the time for protection.

The stove was still roaring full blast and I decided to thaw out my clothes. I tied a thin cord across the tent roof to hang my jacket, mask, and outer gloves on, then slid the end of the sleeping pad on which the burning stove sat directly underneath the clothing. It worked rather well until the melted ice began to drip down onto the stove, threatening to extinguish it. But after a little adjustment all was fine. My tent was just big enough for me, Charlie, and my equipment. When the stove was going, I had to be careful not to tip it over. A tent fire out here would be disastrous. Not only could I lose my shelter, but I could be injured or killed, as many others have been.

I had time to clean house. All the diving in and out of the tent door had allowed unwanted snow in. I hadn't brought a tent brush with me. I made an entry in my journal, "Next trip bring a small tent brush." I tried using an extra pair of gloves as a brush, but they didn't work very well because I had to thaw them out afterward, which used extra fuel. Fuel consumption was important. I had an extra five gallons of white-gas on the sled but I wanted to keep it in case of an emergency.

As my clothes thawed out, an ice fog caused by the steam formed inside the tent, attached itself to the ceiling, and clung there like frost. Each time an extra-strong blast of wind shook the tent the frost fell like snow. Sitting there, listening to the wind flap and shake the tent, I felt vulnerable and insignificant. As I waited out the storm in a shelter with walls thin enough to see through, life beyond the storm seemed remote and no longer a part of me. Home was another planet. Family and friends couldn't help me here. No use thinking about them. I even tried not to think of my surroundings outside the tent walls. I didn't really want to know what was out there. It was too much to grasp all at once. It was better to concentrate on my own tiny world inside the tent.

My clothing had thawed out and I turned off the stove. With its loud roar silenced, there was only the wind and flapping tent to listen to. It was almost noon, but time was related directly to the storm. When it stopped we could go. Until then the wind was in control. Charlie had the right idea. He hadn't stirred all morning. He was sleeping the storm away. I snuggled down deep inside my sleeping bag, retreating into my own world of warmth, and I too fell asleep.

When I woke again at 5:00 P.M., the wind was still raging. The back of the tent was facing into the wind and was pushing inward from the weight of snow building up on the outside. I put my feet against the inside wall and tried to push the snow load off the outside. Most of it fell away. Then I noticed the wind was forcing snow up under the tent fly and pressure was building up against the main tent wall. I was worried that the extra weight might tear the seams out and the tent would blow apart. If that happened, I would have to use my sled as shelter. It would be difficult and marginal because of the lack of space, but I would have no alternative in an emergency.

I knew I would have to go outside to check the radio antenna and the tent. I tried to put it off by thinking of a reason why I shouldn't do it, but there wasn't one. So with great reluctance I crawled out of my warm cocoon and reached for my jacket. At least I could zip it up now. I pulled my hat down low and put on goggles. Then I reached a gloved hand out with the anemometer to measure the wind speed. A steady forty miles per hour with gusts to forty-six. The temperature was minus 19 degrees. I felt discouraged. How long would this go on? Springtime storms from the south can be long and fierce.

I eased myself outside, trying not to let snow into the tent. It blew in anyway. When I turned into the wind to look for the antenna at the back of the tent, I was almost thrown off my feet. Lowering my chin to my chest and hunching my shoulders, I crouched low, but the wind still tossed me around so I quickly dropped into a crawl, keeping a tight grip on the tie-down ropes as I worked my way around the tent. The blowing snow was rammed into my face and body. Breathing was impossible. The air was sucked away each time I faced the wind.

I finally reached the back of the tent and was relieved to find the antenna still there and stretched out in place. Then I crawled around the back of the tent, pushing up snow to fill the gap at the bottom of the fly and block the blowing snow that was building up pressure on the inner wall. The fine, light snow was impossible to pack. I piled some up, then moved on, hoping it would do. My back was to the wind now as I reached the other side of the tent, and it drove the cold deep into my flesh. I hurried to check out the rest of the tie-downs and scrambled back into the tent.

Shivering, I quickly exchanged my jacket for the down parka and sat huddled on my sleeping bag trying to get warm. A long hot drink from my thermos slowly brought life back to my cold body. I added hot water from another thermos to a bowl of instant rice. Dessert was some walnuts and cashew nuts.

As I had dashed through the doorway I stumbled over Charlie and he woke up. He had stretched, yawned, and now he was sitting beside the closed door waiting for me to unzip it. I reached over and opened it just wide enough for him to crawl through. He looked out and quickly pulled his head back in. For a moment he stared through the opening, then with obvious reluctance went outside to attend the call of nature. It was a quick call. He was back in no time, covered with snow, which he proceeded to shake off in a great shower that flew all over the place, even onto my sleeping bag. He picked at the dog food I had laid out for him, then crunched up a handful of crackers, and with a loud, contented groan settled down to resume the business of sleeping out the storm.

It was only seven-thirty. I had nothing else to do so I decided to call base early. "The high winds will last one or two more days," Terry told me. "We have bad weather here too. Sorry I don't have better news for you." Trying to sound cheerful I replied, "No problem, we can sit it out." I signed off feeling less optimistic than I had pretended to be. But my body was returning to life again with the help of my cozy parka. So I decided to do as Charlie was doing—go to sleep and forget about the storm until morning.

DAY 10

Each time I woke during the night the wind was still tearing at the tent walls. When I woke again at about 8:00 A.M., I just lay there thinking of the miles I could have traveled by now. There was nothing to do but ponder my predicament.

I know that springtime storms in the Arctic can be severe. During the winter a high-pressure system sits over the geographic North Pole and spreads throughout the polar region. Springtime brings south winds and warmer temperatures. The resulting storms with high winds can be extreme and long lasting. Unlike the mountains there is nowhere on the ice pack to hide. The snow isn't deep enough to dig a snow cave and the only shelter is behind a pressure ridge, which is definitely not a safe place to be if the floating ice pack decides to move. Pressure ridges are created when the leading edges of ice floes crash together in high winds, with the edges pushed upward by the colossal grinding power of the moving ice. But the ridge can also pull apart at any time, leaving a long, wide strip of open water. In a storm the best camping place is in the middle of a flat area of older, thick ice, with no apparent cracking or ridging. Even there, the ice can unexpectedly crack apart or, under extreme pressure, heave and move to create a new ridge.

Survival in an Arctic storm depends on finding shelter. Large squares or oblong blocks cut from wind-packed snow make good windbreaks. This form of shelter is commonly used in the mountains. However, the light snowfall of the Arctic along the route to the magnetic North Pole causes a scarcity of packed snow deep enough to cut blocks from. Sea ice is sometimes used as an alternative. But compacted, rock-hard sea ice is difficult to saw through and doing so consumes vast amounts of energy, especially if it is multiyear ice, the form of ice that has remained unmelted for more than two years.

The Eskimo igloo made of snow blocks was the classic Arctic shelter until it became obsolete after the arrival of the snowmobile. The Inuit and others who inhabit the polar regions hunt mostly by snowmobile these days. They can leave a settlement by snowmobile for a day's hunting in a favorite area and return within twenty-four hours. For longer hunts, pitching tents has become common. A sturdy, low-profile tent, built to shed the wind and anchored all around to the ice with metal ice screws, is a dependable shelter on the Arctic sea ice.

So far, my tent had survived the savagery of this storm, which at 9:00 A.M. showed no sign of easing. The snow was still piled up outside at the end of the tent but not enough to cause a problem. From the inside, it looked well anchored, so I decided against another inspection. I listlessly ate breakfast and worried about polar bears and lost travel time.

It seemed reasonable to assume that polar bears wouldn't be so apt to hunt in this weather, but I wasn't sure. I was a sitting duck if one did come by. The wind would hide any sound of an approaching bear and Charlie might not sense one unless we were downwind. If only I knew how long this wretched wind was going to last. I felt imprisoned in a tiny cell just a few feet wide, surrounded by an impenetrable wall of snow that raced through the air like pellets. My jailer, the howling wind, would prevent me from moving until, in its own time, it stopped.

I was sitting in my sleeping bag with my map spread across my knees, wondering how I could make up for lost time once we resumed our journey, when I was suddenly jolted by the sound of a loud crack outside the tent. The map flew in one direction and the sleeping bag in another as I jumped up, grabbed the rifle, and unzipped the door. I could see nothing through the blowing snow. I waited tensely, crouched in the doorway trying to keep out of the wind. Surely a bear couldn't make a sound that loud, I thought. Charlie had jumped up as fast as I had, moving from the porch into the tent area. He, too, was alert and tense, but not as if there was a bear close by. What was going on?

In another moment I had my answer. My whole body jumped in fright when once more an ear-splitting crack rent the air. For an instant, just as I heard the sound, I saw a crack slice through the ice five feet in front of the tent. Now it dawned on me what was happening. Just as I knew it could, the storm was causing the ice pack to move, and subjected to great tension, it was splitting open. Grabbing my jacket, hat, and goggles, I went outside and half crouched, half crawled to the crack. It was three inches wide, beginning and ending somewhere out there in the blowing snow. With relief I noticed that it wasn't widening. I saw the second crack six feet beyond the first one. It was a little wider but it wasn't changing width either.

At least it wasn't a polar bear, I thought. But what was happening to the ice around me? Terrified that it seemed to be breaking up, I hurried back to the tent and packed everything in case the ice began to seriously disintegrate around and even under my tent. At least if the need arose, I could get out fast and keep my equipment from going into the water.

The boredom of sitting out the storm had left in an instant and now I was fueled by fear again as I quickly packed up. Charlie was on his feet looking anxious. The sound of the breaking ice had scared him, too. I crouched outside the door, dug the sled out from under two feet of snow, and pulled it into the tent. It was crowded, but I could pack it there and be ready to go. Charlie was alert and sat in the back of the tent watching. Then I remembered his sled. It had most of his dog food on it. Out I went again into the howling wind, dug it out, and pulled it close to the tent door. I finished packing and then dressed. Charlie already had his sled harness on. It was a comfortable one so he wore it all the time. We were both set to go at a moment's notice. But all we could do now was wait to see what would happen.

I was about a half mile out from the Bathurst shoreline. The storm might be pulling the sea ice temporarily away from the shore ice, or the winds could be pushing the sea ice along the coastline, causing it to split where the sea and shore ice met. I felt reasonably confident that the splits wouldn't develop into wide leads of open water because I hadn't seen any leads as I skied over the ice. Wide leads don't normally develop in this area, although I was on the edge of Penny Strait, which is the body of water flowing from the northern shores of Bathurst to just north of our position at Sargent Point. The waters of Penny Strait flow swiftly, causing the ice to become unstable and, in places to the north, very thin. This could be an area where strong winds might cause the ice to split and break up more easily than in the southern area I had recently passed through. I hoped we would be safe. Still I couldn't relax. My mind was ready to propel my body into flight if the ice began to disintegrate under the tent. I pulled Charlie close to me. If we had to leave in a hurry, I would get him out with me.

A half hour later I was cramped and cold with inactivity. The wind was as strong as ever and the constant flapping of the tent and the howling wind had become tiresome to listen to. Rummaging in the food bag I found a small bag of walnuts. I offered Charlie some, but he didn't like them so I munched them alone. The ice was less noisy now, the emergency appeared to be over, and I decided it was time to set things up for the night. I was leading Charlie back to his porch when, suddenly, a series of three or four loud riflelike cracks sent me racing with a pounding heart to the doorway to see what was going on. There were no signs of new cracks nearby. But when I scrambled outside I found three new ones that had knifed their way north to south through the ice. The nearest, a pencil-thin line, was only two feet from the side of the tent while the other two were ten feet away and several inches wide. Crouching in the wind, trying to protect myself from the blowing snow that felt like sand blasting my exposed skin, I heard more muffled rifle shots in the distance as the ice pack split open with the violence of the storm.

Quickly returning to the shelter of the tent to escape the wind, I tried to decide what I should do. Poor Charlie was nervous. He wasn't a happy dog. I put my arm around him, trying to reassure him, trying to keep my anxiety from him. My nerves were shattering just like the ice all around me. Would the next crack slice directly under my tent? I wanted to get away from this awful place with its wind and breaking ice, but it was impossible to leave while the storm raged and visibility was reduced to a few feet. All I could do was remain sheltered, stay as warm as possible, and hope for the best. I knew the storm couldn't last forever.

It was almost time for the radio call to base camp. I was anxious to hear another weather forecast. I found the batteries and stuffed them into an inner pocket to warm while I set up the radio on the front end of the sled, hoping the antenna was still up and pointed at base camp. After placing the batteries in the slots in the back of the radio I turned it on. It immediately crackled to life. The reception was good. Terry came on the air anxiously inquiring about the storm. "It's bad out here," I told her matter-of-factly. "What does the weather report say?"

"It should improve tonight," she replied, much to my relief. "Tomorrow will be better. What's Charlie doing?"

"Mostly sleeping," I replied.

"That figures," she said. Then she gave me the good news that the snowmobile expedition had found its way safely back to Polaris. They were abandoning their plans because of the severity of the storm. Terry's voice was always cheerful. She wished us good traveling and we signed off until the following night.

I couldn't sit up all night listening to the cracking ice, so I left the sled packed except for my sleeping equipment. Charlie went back to his porch and curled up. My supper was a few cashew nuts and a hot drink from my thermos. I didn't dare light the stove. I wouldn't be able to hear the ice over its noisy roar, and a lit stove would be one more problem if we had to leave the tent in a hurry.

Unable to resist taking another look at the ice cracks to check their stability, I donned hat and jacket and hurried outside. The closest crack at the front of the tent had widened to six or seven inches but the second one had closed up. The pencil-line split at the side of the tent was now almost a foot across and the rest were either closed or just a little wider than before. The ice was still moving.

I scrambled back through the wind and snow to the tent and decided to sleep in all of my clothes and my boots just in case. I pulled my sleeping bag close to Charlie where I could grab him quickly. My greatest fear now was that the ice might split apart under the tent. A gap wide enough to allow us to fall into the freezing water could end the expedition on the spot.

Sleep was important before a long, hard day tomorrow, but my heart really wasn't in it. I lay partly inside the sleeping bag dozing off, only to wake up listening, straining to hear the ice pack above the howl of the wind. About midnight the wind began to lessen. The high-pitched howl was gone and the tent walls were quieter. My prayers were being answered. The storm was moving on. At 2:00 A.M. I took a hopeful look out the door. The wind was blowing at half its former strength, but was still so strong I couldn't see through the swirling snow. I returned to a tense, restless doze waiting for improved visibility, longing to get out of there to a place that wasn't breaking up around me.

5.

THIN ICE

DAY 11

≡ The wind continued to slacken, but it wasn't until six that I could see far enough ahead to travel safely. A heavy ice fog had developed in the early hours of the morning, but by six had thinned so that visibility was about a quarter of a mile. I had been afraid to leave any sooner. The ice pack was too broken up to risk traveling. But now the wind, our captor, was gone, the doors of our prison had been flung open, and we were free to go.

Charlie appeared more than ready to move on. He had also been restless during the night, getting up and turning in tight circles to make a "nest" before lying down again, curled up in a ball. I was already packed, so after a handful of crackers and walnuts for me and dog food for Charlie we left. The minus 15 degrees was more comfortable than the lower temperatures of the first few days, but I felt uneasy about it. Did it mean another storm was on the way? And the wind, although now slight, was still from the south, which meant the weather was unsettled enough to bring another storm.

The sun shone thinly through the light ice fog. The blowing snow had drifted and was packed tightly into low ridges from a few inches to two feet high. Looking anxiously around for signs of cracks, I saw numerous pencil-thin lines across the ice and several gaps up to three inches across. We arrived at the first of these gaps and Charlie stepped carefully to the edge, looked down at the cold, black water, paused a moment, then stepped nervously across, watching the water beneath him. "It's all right, Charlie," I said, using my most encouraging tone of voice. He obviously didn't like to step across water, but by now he had gained confidence in me and was willing to trust my judgment.

After twenty minutes of careful travel, we came to a particularly fractured area with wide gaps almost three feet across, stretching east to west across our path. I looked down into the inky blackness of the water and shuddered, thinking of what it would be like to fall in. The sudden cold shock would be paralyzing, perhaps fatal. I had visions of the horrible stories I had been told of sled dogs that fell in the water and were cut loose to prevent them from pulling the rest of the team in with them. Sometimes they scrambled out, but if the currents were strong they disappeared under the ice. No wonder Charlie was so cautious around open water. He knew the consequences of falling in.

Looking ahead at the maze of cracks and gaps we would have to find a safe way through, I was struck by a dark thought. If I made a mistake and Charlie or I fell in the water, his trust in me would be for nothing. When we began this journey, he was an Inuit dog, accustomed to a life devoid of human kindness. He learned, as all Inuit dogs do, to be careful around humans. After all, the slightest infraction could at the very least bring a swift kick to the ribs, while a moderate mistake could end in death. Charlie certainly had no reason to trust a human with his life. But he trusted me.

He stood now, leaning lightly against my right leg, waiting for me to decide what to do. He had developed this habit of light contact when he was around open water or was unsure of my next move, and I had learned to give him definite body signals to indicate the plan ahead. His "What do we do next?" reaction was very different from his confident, in-control, protective, go-get-em polar bear stance. As I patted his head he looked up at me, his love and trust showing in his dark eyes. Quickly bending down I hugged him tightly. The thought of any harm coming to Charlie felt like a lead weight on my shoulders. I loved this big, black, furry dog, and somehow we would get through safely to the pole. It was a precious gift to be trusted and loved by a dog that had never learned trust and had never known human kindness.

Once more I looked ahead at the fractured ice, trying to see a way through without having to go a long way around. I was surprised at the thinness of the ice pack. Only one to two feet thick, it was several feet thinner than the ice we had traveled over the last few days, which explained why it had fractured under the stress of the storm.

All at once the ice began to move again, cracking and grinding in all directions. I stood terrified as the gap in front of me slowly closed to only inches. The winds of the past two days combined with the tides were still moving the ice pack. Quickly taking advantage of the now-narrow split, we stepped over. The next gap, a few yards away, was wider and slowly opening. I grabbed Charlie, urging him to hurry, and we scrambled over that one too. But then there was a sharp bang and a crack raced through the ice just inches in front of my ski tips. My mouth was dry with fear. I wanted out of here and fast. We crossed the new split only to reach the edge of a gap three feet across. I was afraid it would suddenly widen. To allow Charlie to jump without the traces of his sled pulling him backward, I quickly attached his sled to a long rope. His head cocked with uncertainty, he watched me approach the crack. My skis, although bending alarmingly in the middle, reached across the gap and I stepped across, pulling my sled over after me.

Poor Charlie felt this was the limit. A few inches were all right, but this? I leaned toward him with my hand outstretched, calling his name, trying to sound calm and confident. After a few moments staring down at the dreaded water, he jumped. His powerful body sailed over gracefully and easily. I patted and fussed over him to show how impressed I was. Looking pleased with himself, he responded to my big hug with a lick across my face, which I interpreted as a kiss. All I had to do now was pull his sled over.

The ice fog was rapidly disappearing, making it easy to see the ice surface ahead. I stopped to listen. The ice was silent again. Perhaps we had experienced its last convulsion. I hoped so. We passed over several more splits and gaps, the widest no more than three feet across. Charlie was doing fine. I had tied his sled behind mine. My pulling his sled made it easier for him to jump across the gaps. He walked at my side, trusting me completely as we wound our way through the fractured ice. After a few more jumps he didn't even hesitate, sometimes even jumping ahead of me. His confidence improved with every leap. I depended on Charlie to warn me of polar bears, while he relied on my confidence to help him cross open water.

Traversing a patch of innocent-looking wind-packed snow, my skis, sled, and Charlie made it over, but his sled suddenly sank through, leaving the end dangling in open water. I took my skis off to make it easier to go back to lift his sled out, but my right foot almost immediately broke through the crust of snow and my leg plunged in up to my hip, sending panic surging through my body. My foot was in water but my waterproof boot saved it from getting wet. Carefully levering myself out, I went another few cautious paces back to Charlie's sled. I tugged it out of the water, then gingerly made my way back to my skis, put them on and, with even greater care, went forward again. It was safer for me to wear my skis. They were long enough to spread my weight over a larger area, preventing me from punching through the snow that sometimes covered hidden cracks. I shortened Charlie's chain, keeping him close to me in case he went through and needed help.

After a mile we again stood on thicker ice, which appeared to be in one piece. By a stroke of bad luck, the storm had apparently stopped us in an area of thin ice, which was easily moved and broken up by the strong winds. I suspected that the tides this close to the coast and the strong currents that swept around Sargent

Point, in addition to our being a little south of the swift waters of Penny Strait, had all contributed to the unusually thin layer of ice. Whatever the reason, I was so glad we had made it safely across that hazardous area that I didn't even stop to rest or eat. I quickly untied Charlie's sled from mine and attached it to his harness. I was interested in getting as far from there as possible.

With the low, flat, frigid plain of Sargent Point behind us, the coastline of Bathurst Island quickly steepened to an elevation of one hundred feet. The low cliffs were bare and rounded and long stretches of frozen gravel showed through the ice, worn smooth by winds that swept uninterrupted across the bleak terrain. The land ice and sea ice joined to form an enormous, empty, white world all around me so vast that it threatened to engulf my thoughts and myself. The lack of deep color contrast in the white glare took away my sense of scale. I was a tiny, insignificant speck in an enormous emptiness. I wanted to get away to a place where I was no longer dwarfed by my surroundings.

As I passed the cliffs, now to my left, they looked steeper than they really were. I skied away from the coast so that I no longer felt crushed and dwarfed by their size. The flat sea ice ahead of me was vast and empty, in contrast to the coastline cliffs, which loomed over me with their magnified size. Both were intimidating. Traveling alone in such boundless space, devoid of familiar sights and sounds, created in me an acute awareness of my feelings and a heightened sensitivity to my surroundings. My senses didn't talk to me, they screamed. Every part of me was ready to react instantly.

The ever-present mind-numbing fear of polar bears traveled at my shoulder, never letting go. I was by now dealing with one day at a time, and whenever I knew a bear might be close by, or whenever I crossed several fairly fresh tracks, I dealt with only an hour at a time. It was better not to think of the whole journey. One step at a time takes a climber to the top of the mountain and so would one hour at a time take me to the pole. I knew now that I could reach my destination. I felt the only thing that could stop me would be injury or death from a polar bear attack.

I soon saw another flat plain to my left, this one only a half mile long. My map showed an unnamed river meeting the sea at this point, but it was invisible under a mantle of ice. It was ten o'clock and although we had been slow traveling through the area of thin, broken ice we were making good time. I sat on my sled to eat a snack, but as soon as I took the daily food bag from my sled, Charlie made it known with a lot of bouncing and tail wagging that he would enjoy that too. I gave him some dog food, which he ignored as he watched to see what I was going to eat. Sure enough, my food had a much tastier look than his. But I stood my ground and insisted that he eat his food first. When he refused, I sat down on my sled, looking into the distance, making a dramatic show of ignoring him. He got the message and ate every piece of his food before again turning his attention to my crackers and walnuts. After bypassing the walnuts, as usual, he begged for crackers. I gave him two and quickly ate the last three, making it impossible for him to persuade me to give them up. Every day eating had become more of a tactical game, with me coming out the loser. Charlie was such a skillful beggar that he was beginning to eat more of my crackers than I was. So before things got completely out of hand, I resolved to enforce the new rules. Charlie had to eat his food before he could share mine. I was mildly surprised to find that it had worked and I had won the first food battle of the day.

Studying the map for a few moments before starting off again, I tried to determine how far out from the coast we should travel. Three miles east of Bathurst were three tiny specks of land no more than a half mile long called the Cheyne Islands. The large Cheyne River spilled out from the coastline opposite the middle island. In the distance I could see a jagged line of rough ice and guessed it to be caused by the islands and river mouth. I decided on a northerly course two and a half miles out from the coast. My theory was that the ice was probably going to be rougher closer to the river mouth than to the islands. Therefore I would stay away from the coast, but still keep the islands a half mile to my right.

We started off and I noticed that the wind, gusting up to ten miles an hour, still swept across the ice from the south. In a half hour we were opposite South Cheyne Island. All that showed above the ice piled up around its shores was a tiny bit of land no more than two hundred yards long, perhaps fifty yards wide, and according to my map, five feet high. Its surface was black and gravelly, a stark contrast to the glittering white ice that surrounded it. Like a black slash, the island pointed north. Closer to the island the ice sounds grew louder and the smooth ice surface turned to rubble. Long-drawn-out groans mixed with high-pitched squeaks rose from beneath my feet as the ice moved with the fast-flowing currents that squeezed between the three islands and the Bathurst coast.

We crossed a set of fresh polar bear tracks and Charlie wanted to follow them. With his black nose pressed down hard on the ice, he plunged ahead, pulling me with him. The tracks went north in the direction we were traveling in, but I had no desire to catch up with a bear. As far as I was concerned any bear was very welcome to travel without the pleasure of our company. Pulling back on Charlie's leash, I told him to stop, but his momentum made his sled slide past me, careen sideways off a two-foot-high chunk of ice, and dash across my ski tips. It had the effect of suddenly slamming the brakes on my skis, pitching me forward over my ski tips. I landed on my face in a tangle of ski poles and skis. I looked up and there was Charlie gazing back at me. His puzzled expression clearly said, "What on earth are you doing now?"

It was not a happy moment. To begin with, I wasn't in the best defensive position should a bear decide to investigate. Having my face rammed into the ice wasn't a lot of fun either and I could feel the anger rising. Then I remembered how guilty I had felt after I became angry with Charlie just the other day. With a large measure of self-control I kept a firm hand on my feelings while I attempted to untangle my body, skis, and poles. After all, I reminded myself, it's the most natural thing in the world for Charlie to want to chase polar bears. However, I wished he wouldn't do it while pulling his sled. The only way to untangle myself successfully was to release my skis and sled harness. Charlie seemed unaware that he had been the cause of the commotion and lay comfortably down on the ice, resting, while I got myself together again.

We were already stopped, so I decided we might as well eat another bite before moving on. We enjoyed a snack of three peanut butter cups each, then it was time to leave. Charlie, as strong as ever, striding alongside me, calm and confident, showed no sign of fatigue. His character was solid, dependable, and loving. He clearly enjoyed our friendship and the attention I gave him. We had been through all sorts of adventures together and our mutual understanding had grown each day. He was even used to being called by his name. It was hard to believe that two weeks ago he hadn't even had a name.

We set out again, and passing the river outlet I looked ahead trying to find an easy corridor through the ice rubble. To the left, the coast curved sharply inland to form Reindeer Bay, which led to a three-mile stretch of low-lying coastline. To the right we passed the remaining two islands in the Cheyne group. They were much like the first, tiny, low, and black. The middle one was almost invisible, while the third barely showed through the ice.

I noticed several bear tracks going in all directions. Some were windblown, weathered tracks, while others were only a day old. One set we had seen earlier was very fresh, made no more than an hour before. The wind hadn't had time to smooth the edges of the prints. They were large, probably left by a male going north ahead of us. There was no way of telling if the bear, which was downwind of us, would catch our scent and wait for us, hidden in the rubble ice. I skied slowly, straining to see as far ahead as possible through the early afternoon glare.

Charlie suddenly became interested in another set of tracks, this time of a female with two cubs, their prints following close behind the larger ones of their mother. They came from the coast and were fresher than the male tracks ahead of them. Charlie was having a field day, his nose working overtime. I skied another hundred yards, then stopped when I saw the female's tracks turn back in our direction for twenty yards before going on ahead of us again. Looking around nervously I saw no bears and carefully went forward, keeping a close watch. Meanwhile, Charlie had stopped trying to chase tracks and became alert and tense.

It appeared as if the female, catching our scent, had left her cubs briefly and turned back to investigate before continuing north ahead of us. Had she seen us? How far ahead was she? The prints were so fresh that I was certain the bear and cubs were only a few hundred yards away. The ten-mile-an-hour wind was blowing our scent toward her, so assuming we had been seen, I skied on cautiously, peering through the bright glare trying to find the now-familiar creamy white color of an adult bear. The old terror returned. My nerves still hadn't recovered from our flight over cracking ice that morning and I wasn't ready to face a bear.

Charlie walked slightly in front of me, a position he automatically took when a bear was close. When he began a low quiet growl I wondered with growing fear if the bear had stopped again. Ice cubes were sitting in the pit of my stomach and my heart was pounding. If I continued forward I might be ambushed. I couldn't depend on waiting her out. Bears are very patient animals. I needed a new plan.

I decided to ski toward Bathurst and look for a passable overland route along the coast. I was going on the assumption that the bear would be hunting for seals and had no reason to hunt on land. Of course, it would be difficult to pull my sled over the exposed gravel on the land, but it was worth a try. I had no desire to play hide-and-seek with a polar bear in the icy rubble we were traveling through. I could easily become the loser in such a game.

We were almost opposite the northern tip of the flat

coastline of Reindeer Bay. I skied as fast as I could, with frequent nervous glances over my shoulder, while Charlie kept sniffing the air, his black nose held high to catch the bear scent behind us. We were soon close to the coast and there appeared an easy way up onto the flat area of northern Reindeer Bay. I headed for it, happy to see no gravel bars. In fact, there was a reasonably uninterrupted blanket of ice stretching over the land, making it appear very skiable. The shore ice was crunchy and split easily as I put my weight on it, but it was safe. A gently sloping shore greeted us as we climbed up onto land. After so many days it was good to stand on solid land, something that wasn't floating.

Traveling north again we crossed snow-covered gravel bars deposited by river waters during the short Arctic summers and reached the south bank of an unnamed river that flowed into the sea at this point. Our next task was to cross the frozen riverbed. Two hundred yards upriver I found an easy, sloping snow ramp, which dropped ten feet down to the river bottom. I knew my sled would run over me if I pulled it down, so I turned it around and slowly lowered it in front of me. After I had lowered Charlie's sled the same way, we started across, only to find ourselves in loose, powdery snow several feet deep. I immediately sank down to my hips while poor Charlie was almost over his head. Keeping a tight hold on his collar I lifted him, helping him stay on the surface. Fortunately, the river bottom was only a few yards wide at this spot, and after a great deal of huffing, puffing, and stumbling we were across.

Charlie took it all in good humor, although he probably wondered why we didn't stay on the sea ice where he could walk without floundering around in soft snow. I dusted a thick layer of snow off my clothing. Some had found its way beneath my hood to form a cold necklace that slowly melted in tiny rivulets down my neck. Charlie soon rid himself of his layer of unwanted snow with a tremendous shake of his long, thick coat, sending a snow shower all over me. I turned away, but not in time to miss the full blast. "Thank you, Charlie," I said.

Four-hundred-foot Greenwich Hill was a mile and a half north of us on the coast, so rather than climb over the summit, I elected to travel inland northwest in order to skirt the steepest part. Even so, my map showed we had a long steady climb in front of us. As I considered the route I hoped my decision to travel on land had been a good one, but when I remembered the possibility of encountering a waiting bear on the sea ice, the climb ahead suddenly appeared far more attractive.

Our route began over almost flat, snow-covered gravel bars, then steepened quickly to two hundred feet. I climbed diagonally up the slope, my sled dragging behind me over a layer of hard-packed snow that was plastered to the slope by the wind. Fifty feet up the slope I stopped to take off my skis. The snow layer seemed thin and hard enough to make my boots more useful than skis. I grabbed the sled hauling ropes tightly and reached for my ice axe to anchor the sled to the steep slope. One slip and my sled and I would go crashing to the river bottom. Winding the ropes around the metal shaft, I dug the axe into the hard snow as far as it could go. Charlie's sled, only four feet long and now about sixty-five pounds, held easily. I fitted skis and poles along the top of my sled and secured them with two tie-down straps. Then, with my ice axe in my right hand, I turned once more to begin climbing the slope.

It was hard work. I was used to having the sled on

the same level with me, but now it hung below me on the steep slope, forcing me to pull as hard as I could. I used my ice axe for balance and dug my boot edges into the hard snow to make solid steps. My lower leg muscles were burning as I reached the two-hundred-foot level. The slope above was a little less steep and led up to a narrow, flattened ledge. Plodding steadily on, feeling the weight of my sled behind me, I didn't stop until I reached the small, almost flat spot. But it was too cold and windy to stop for long, so on Charlie and I went, slowly gaining elevation, the sled runners squeaking in the dry snow behind us. Charlie, at my side, pulled his sled seemingly without effort. At three hundred feet I stopped climbing and skirted the western flank of Greenwich Hill, still one hundred feet below the summit. I hoped to find a suitable place to look out over the sea ice to see the bears we had tried to avoid, but the land formed a wall between us and the coast.

Instead, I looked west across the island upon a totally different scene from the one in which I had traveled for the past eleven days. The heatless sun shone from a clear sky, the wind was brisk, bone-chilling cold, and the view was panoramic. Glistening white, rounded, rolling hills and shallow valleys stretched as far as I could see. Tucked into the little valleys were tiny, pancake-shaped lakes, frozen solid. Empty of humans and all signs of humanity, there was only the land and the sky, nothing in between. Scale and definition returned. The hills had a different character from the valleys, and the lakes, although frozen white, stood out like ships on the sea. I felt different up there. I was as large as life, a significant human being again.

It was too cold to stand for long. I was beginning to shiver. The increased elevation also increased our exposure to the wind. Turning our backs to the south wind, Charlie and I resumed our journey north. Without skis my boots squeaked loudly on snow so dry that a shovelful yields only drops of water instead of cupfuls. I was walking a trackless land just as I had skied the trackless ocean of ice we had temporarily left. I followed a route over the hills that allowed me to pull my sled most of the time. It was only occasionally, on the steeper downhill sections, that I had to lower it in front of me.

At three o'clock, with the sun swinging southwest behind us, it was time to decide whether I should camp on the island or return to the sea ice. On the island I had fewer bear problems. Normally bears use the land only as a crossing point to hunt seals on the sea ice. But I never knew when I would reach an area of exposed gravel too difficult to pull my sled over. The wind was another factor in my planning. The added elevation in a high wind storm could prove dangerous. As a test I had already tried to sink a tent anchor into the frozen, rocky gravel. After fifteen minutes of vigorous digging it had penetrated only a half inch, and I gave up, realizing how impossible it would be to anchor my tent on land in high winds. Climbing up and down hills using valuable energy and time was another disadvantage of staying on land. So I decided to return to the sea ice at the first easy downward slope to the coast.

Soon I saw a long, deep slash pointing east, dividing the valley ahead. It was Green River. After a long, twisting route through the interior hills, it worked its way to the sea at Paine Point. "Charlie," I said, "here's our road to the sea. We'll follow the river down." But the closer we got the less inviting it looked. There was no way down. The river was banked by hundred-foot cliffs that formed an enormous dark brown gorge, towering silently over the frozen river below. My map showed the gorge to be two miles long, after which the river snaked east across a low, wide plain to the sea. To the west, a half mile farther inland beyond the gorge, the map showed a fork in the river where the contour lines indicated a gradual slope down into the river.

When I looked down at that great forbidding gorge and the narrow white ribbon of frozen water twisting through the bottom, I gave up my idea of traveling a river road to the coast. There might be unknowns down there, and once deep in the gorge I would be trapped. I felt safer with space around me in which I could maneuver if need be. Disappointed, I turned away from the coast and wearily trudged slowly upward, looking for the river fork. Just as the map promised, there it was. And a few yards ahead I found a good place to cross.

While I lowered the two sleds to the bottom, Charlie, who was on a thirty-foot rope, began to descend by the orthodox method of walking, but a steep icy patch suddenly sent him flying to land spread-eagled at the bottom. Looking up at me with a mildly surprised expression, he shook himself, then apparently reached the conclusion that this was fun. Scrambling to the top again, leaving claw marks in the ice behind him, he promptly turned, dropped to the ice on his belly and with feet straight out in front slid down again. Standing open-mouthed, I watched this canine version of sledding with astonishment.

The sleds were already down as Charlie, like an excited child on a family picnic, returned to the top for his third sliding trip. I decided to join the fun. Besides, it appeared to be the best way down. Sitting, I started sliding downward on my seat with Charlie sliding alongside, but halfway down the hill our routes crossed and we landed at the bottom in a pile of tangled bodies. I got to my feet as Charlie, still in a playful mood, flipped himself over, squirming and scratching his back on the hard ice, inviting me to scratch his tummy. We both temporarily forgot the long day and our tired bodies.

The snow at this crossing, unlike the last one, was wind-packed and solid, but another long, steep, two-hundred-foot climb faced us on the other side. It would take us up to a wide, windswept plateau called Organ Heights, which, according to the map, should have a reasonable two-hundred-foot slope down its eastern flank to the coast. I was rapidly growing bone weary of pulling my sled up and down hills, and Charlie, who had left his playful mood back at the last crossing, was now lying down to rest at every opportunity, waiting until the last moment before reluctantly getting to his feet to continue. His message was clear: "When do we camp?" This extraordinary day of broken sea ice, polar bears, and land travel, walking up and down hills pulling a sled that had become an extension of my body, seemed several years long. I hated to tell Charlie to keep going, and it must have been puzzling to him to try to figure out why we couldn't stop. But we had to force our tired bodies to keep plodding on until we came to a camping place on the sea ice.

It was 5:30 P.M. and we still had to find our way down to the coast before looking for a camping spot. Standing in the chilling wind, high on the two-hundred-foot plateau, I looked across the white blanket of ice that stretched thirty miles across Penny Strait to Devon Island in the distance. With high, rugged mountains and coastline, Devon was a contrast to the low-lying islands I had so far passed on my journey. I could see Hyde

Parker Island about halfway across the strait. It appeared to have a long, narrow peninsula, pointing like a slate-gray finger to the north. Beyond Hyde Parker was an almost square island called Isle of Mists, but I could see no sign of mist as I looked across. At base camp I had been warned of the swift currents, thin ice, and possible open patches of water in Penny Strait, which are caused by currents sweeping through a narrow channel around the northern coast of Bathurst. I scanned the ice, looking for dark patches of open water. My search stopped at a fog bank rising high above the inky blackness of an area of open water many miles southeast.

These large open areas of water, known as *polynyas*, only recently understood by scientists, meet the cooler Arctic air to form a thick fog bank. Polynyas, which normally stay ice-free all year round due to a unique combination of currents, wind, and upwellings, provide a feeding haven for overwintering mammals and birds —a biological Arctic paradise. The polynya I saw now sat a long way off my route, presenting no problem. Of greater concern were several large gray patches to the north, some close to the coast and at least fifty feet across, which signaled thin, new ice. My route wound through that patchwork quilt of gray and white. However, the gray areas were spread far apart. Perhaps I could skirt the edges, keeping to the thicker white ice.

When at last I found a long, steep slope descending to the coast, I turned my sled around and tied Charlie's sled to it. Then, with Charlie at my side, I held the hauling ropes tightly, braking both sleds as they slid backward halfway down the slope. There the surface changed to a layer of small gray rocks with rough, sharp surfaces. The sleds refused to slide so I resorted to pushing them downward, trying to avoid rocks that scratched long grooves on the bottom surface of the runners. Rather than damage the runners, I turned the sleds and traversed the hill, seeking a place to lower them over a smoother surface. Three hundred yards away I found smoother gravel, and again acting as a brake, I lowered the sleds slowly down the long gravelly slope to the icy shoreline.

Although the sea ice meant polar bears, open water, and rough surfaces, I was glad to return. In spite of the hazards, it was a highway compared to the hills and deep gorges of the island we had left behind. Traveling overland on foot, pulling a sled, meant too many detours and energy-consuming time. Now, with Charlie again pulling his own sled, we moved easily through the fragile, thinner shore ice to safer, smooth ice half a mile offshore. At last a thankful Charlie could rest, while I, no less thankful, stopped for the day to set up camp. We had traveled twenty-seven miles. Even before the tent was erected, Charlie was curled up on the ice asleep. I knew how he felt; I could hardly wait to take off my boots and climb into my sleeping bag.

After twisting the last tent anchor into the ice with hands that, while no worse, had not greatly improved from the frostbite ordeal, I stood up and, as was my usual custom, looked carefully to all sides for polar bears. But something else caught my eye: lenticular clouds, saucer-shaped and suspended against the pale blue space that stretched to infinity above them. I had often encountered lenticulars in the mountains. They mean only one thing, an incoming storm with extreme winds. One look at those clouds was enough to make me dig deeply into reserves of energy that had somehow escaped use during the day. I hurried to unpack and set up camp, stowing everything, including my skis, in my tightly lashed-down sled or in the tent. Then I anchored the tent to the ice with every ice screw I had. After satisfying myself that everything was as secure as I could make it, I woke Charlie and to his delight ushered him into the tent vestibule with his pan of food where he happily munched his dinner.

Looking out again, I saw that high-altitude cirrus clouds laden with ice crystals were beginning to move across the sky high above the lenticulars. The south wind picked up to over fifteen miles an hour, kicking snow off the ice. I called base camp and told Terry of the weather change. She said Resolute Bay weather was still stable. After giving her my exact location, I signed off in the hope of sleeping awhile before the storm arrived.

At 9:00 P.M. a chill settled over us as the sun slowly sank below the horizon without really setting, lighting the nights of the twenty-four-hour days that were now following us to the pole. To save time, rather than cook, I snacked on a sparse dinner of nuts, dry granola, and crackers. Then, savoring the moment I had been looking forward to, I climbed wearily into my sleeping bag to end the fifteen-hour day. At my head in the tent porch, Charlie was already sound asleep.

6.

THE VISIT

DAY 12

≡ I awoke at 1:00 A.M. to a howling windstorm that shook the tent. Charlie was curled up, presumably still asleep, undisturbed by the fury unleashed on our tiny home. The end of the tent that pointed into the wind bulged inward under the pressure of wind and snow. Kicking the walls from the inside was no help. I would have to go outside to shovel away the snow that was piling up against the back wall, threatening to collapse the tent.

I struggled into my jacket, fumbling with the zipper, which jammed halfway. The culprit was a small sliver of ice wedged into the zipper teeth. I scraped it off with the fingernail of my unfrostbitten little finger and pulled the zipper to my neck. I made a halfhearted attempt to pull my boots on but gave up when a crack opened up on my right index finger. My camp boots would have to do. Replacing my gloves, I opened the door, stepped over a still-sleeping Charlie into the vestibule, and grabbed my shovel. I cautiously went outside to test the strength of the wind. A high-pitched yowl drove into my mind as I caught the first full blast. When I turned into the wind to scramble around the tent, the wind pushed me back, almost ripping the shovel from my hands as a gust caught the blade. Dropping onto all fours, I crawled to where the snow was thickest against the back outside wall. As the freezing blasts bit into my face, I swept the snow away to the side, releasing the tent wall from its increasing weight. With snow swirling crazily around me, I scrambled back into the tent, glad to be out of the howling gale. My tent not only provided shelter but was my only security in a lonely, insecure world.

I took my jacket off and slid into the warm depths of my sleeping bag. If my tent was my security, my sleeping bag was my cocoon, the only place I could go where everything was warm and friendly. I could pull the bag up over my head and hide from the unrelenting fear of polar bears and the storm that ripped around the tent. I fell into a light sleep, waking often to the sound of the tent shaking in the wind.

At seven o'clock the storm still showed no signs of letting up so I lit my stove to melt ice for breakfast. Charlie woke up, stretched, and looked over my shoulder to see what I was taking out of the food bag. He saw crackers and leaned over to help himself. "No, Charlie!" I said. He hesitated, then turned to his dog food, keeping an eye on me to see what he might steal or beg. After eating half his food he stood, looking sleepy, watching me pour water into my granola. Then, deciding that I was going to keep it all for myself, he turned around and curled up and went back to sleep.

By now my food was monotonous and sometimes disgusting as I became lazy and mixed granola, rice, milk powder, and even a few crackers together. It was filling and served a purpose. Cooking wasn't my favorite camping pastime even on summer hikes in the Cascade Mountains. I often just took a loaf of bread per day and left the whole business of food preparation at that. At home it was different. There I enjoyed planning and cooking meals. But out on the Arctic ice, eating in a cold tent with cold, frostbitten hands was for survival only. There was no real incentive to be creative. Still, as I looked at the lukewarm mess in my bowl, I decided that I should really make an attempt to at least eat things separately. Then, idly pondering the problem, I thought it made some sense to eat one-dish meals. The whole meal is over and done with much faster and with less fiddling around. Having rationalized my lazy cooking habits, I finished the last spoonful and sat back on my sleeping bag to plan the day.

There wasn't much to plan. I couldn't go anywhere in the storm, the tent was tidy, my hands were too sore to mend a rip in one of my gloves, and my only reading material was a tiny New Testament. I passed through the rest of the morning in slow motion, reading and then sleeping. The contrast between travel days, on which I was forever trying to go faster, trying to make as many miles as possible, and a day such as this, on which I was forced into idleness, made me treasure good weather.

Resolute Bay, my base
camp and the place to
which I hoped I would
return safely.

Charlie, eyeing me with
curiosity the day we
met.

Before climbing into my sleeping bag, Charlie and
I always looked around for uninvited dinner
guests in white furry coats.

A polar bear with cubs, I learned on the second
day of our journey, was usually both very hungry
and very aggressive.

RIGHT: Although I had practiced with my rifle, I
hoped I would never have to use it to kill a
polar bear. Charlie was my best protection.

ABOVE: As I trudged across the landscape, I felt dwarfed by the towering pinnacles of ice.

I couldn't cry. Tears would freeze my eyes shut. Everything froze, even breath on my mask.

A full-grown male charging across rough ice was an unwelcome and terrifying sight.

My tent flapped like a
flag when I tried to
put it up in the wind.

Charlie had a little
trick of rubbing up
against my leg to get
a free back scratch
when I skied.

Crossing the rough sea ice south of King Christian Island was slow, arduous, exhausting work.

A huge iceberg south of King Christian Island trapped in the grip of the sea ice.

Head down, tiny black eyes flashing, a polar bear charges with a peculiar pigeon-toed gait.

Charlie posed only very reluctantly for a photograph to mark the most northerly point of our expedition.

Charlie standing guard outside my tent while I
called base camp. Before our journey was over, he
had wormed his way inside to share both my
sleeping bag and my pillow.

Each day of our journey
ended with a hug for
Charlie. He responded by
licking my face—and
begging for my food. He
usually got it.

At noon I heated water for another gourmet delight, followed by hot chocolate. As I filled my vacuum bottles again, I noticed lengthening gaps of silence between the gusts of wind that howled around the tent. The storm was passing, and I packed up just in case it quieted down and I could leave. When I looked out, all I could see was snow being picked up off the ice by the wind and rearranged in ridges around the tent.

At three the wind had gone its way and Charlie and I were bathed in a welcome silence, broken only by the occasional low groan or high-pitched whine from deep within the ice pack beneath my tent. Visibility was no more than a few feet. The air was still but filled with tiny snowflakes floating lazily down to lie quietly on the ice.

Frustration began to set in, even anger at the storm for daring to last this long. How in the world was I ever going to get to the pole? At least during the last storm, I had breaking ice around my tent to keep boredom at bay. I quickly tossed that thought away. I would happily stay bored rather than ever go through that again.

By seven at night the snow had stopped and the air was thick with fog and rising temperatures that now reached plus 9 degrees. I walked away from the tent, trying to decide if I should begin skiing again. I was no more than fifteen feet away when I looked back and I could barely see the tent through the blanket of white that hung like a curtain all around me. I decided to wait until the visibility was a little better.

Back inside the tent I took out my map to study the coastline ahead. I was close to the northern part of Bathurst Island, where I would turn northwest. I remembered the gray patches of new ice I had seen yesterday as I stood high on the cliffs. These patches were ahead of me, unseen in the whiteness that reduced my world to a few feet. I couldn't travel safely until I could see those patches.

I grew more frustrated by the hour. I felt worse sitting there than I had felt struggling through a fifteen-hour day. I was hoping the wind would move around to the north. I had dared to complain about the cold north wind I had been forced to ski into. But at least a northerly wind would bring back good weather. Never again would I complain about it. I kept checking outside, trying to detect even the faintest wind shift to the north. I almost willed the wind to turn. To no avail. My world had been reduced to less than an average-sized living room.

At 8:00 P.M. I told Terry of the temperature increase and asked about the weather forecast. "Last night after your radio call," she said, "the weather office in Resolute called us to warn you of high winds coming to your area. Are you okay?"

"Charlie and I are okay," I replied. "The winds have come and gone. What's the forecast?"

Terry's reply wasn't reassuring. "You might get more wind up there yet."

I closed the radio down and checked outside. No change, but just in case the winds came back as Terry had warned, I checked the tie-down lines and ice screws. Everything was secure and ready. Then I had a flash of what seemed a brilliant idea. I figured that if I took the skins off my skis, I could make up time by traveling faster without the extra drag. Before the storm the ice in this area had looked fast and smooth. I reasoned that with faster skis I would make up some of the time I was losing sitting there. Unlashing the skis from the sled, I sat in the tent doorway pulling the skins off and rolling them up. I was excited that I was doing something to help my forward progress. I had no idea then that I was going to regret that brilliant idea.

I woke Charlie, who looked at his food, pushed it around in his bowl, then sleepily lay down again. I poured warm water from a thermos into his pan but his reaction was total boredom. After several minutes I dumped it out before it froze solid in the pan. That seemed to trigger a signal in Charlie. He suddenly got to his feet, walked to the end of his chain, began digging a shallow hole in the ice, and then ate the fine pieces of ice he dug up. Returning to the tent vestibule he dug another shallow hole in the ice and lay in it.

I knew Charlie had eaten ice all his life and wasn't used to someone offering him bowls of warm water. At the beginning of the expedition, he just looked at the water rather than drink it and it quickly froze in the pan. But I had noticed before leaving base camp that his urine and that of other dogs in the village was a dark, almost orange yellow, indicating they weren't getting enough liquid. I loaded extra fuel onto my sled so I could melt ice for Charlie. He had gradually accepted more water each day during the journey, but still preferred ice. After the eighth day his urine was a lighter color so I knew the extra trouble of melting ice, and figuring out how to get him to drink it before it froze, was paying off.

DAY 13

≡ I slept little after 2:00 A.M. The sound of the wind crept into my sleep as it grew into another howling gale. By four o'clock the tent was shaking in all directions at once. Terry was right, the storm wasn't over yet. I cursed the wind. How dare it come back? Alone in my little world I looked upon the wind and the storm as enemies with no right to intrude into my plans. The worst part was the helplessness, my inability to change things and take control. I had learned to control my emotions when faced with a polar bear, when the ice was breaking all around me, when my hands screamed for relief, and when the loneliness pressed inward. But now Mother Nature was in control and I didn't like it. Then in the midst of my anger and frustration, a glimmer of reason took hold and grew. A new lesson was unfolding. I could take control by staying calm and waiting quietly for the storm to run its course. I would conserve energy, study my maps and navigation for the journey ahead, then leave when Mother Nature gave up. I watched Charlie just sleeping the storm away. He would be rested and ready to go when the time came. He was in control. The Arctic classroom and Charlie were teaching me yet another lesson.

Breakfast was an uninteresting event. Now that I had time on my hands, my food and its shortcomings were more noticeable. When hurrying to leave in the mornings and then at night hurrying to eat and go to sleep, I ate my food without mental comment. Now I decided that I would be selective about what went into the bowl and what I mixed with it. That morning's mix of granola, milk powder, a chunk of butter, peanut butter cups, coconut, and crackers was not the way to start a day of patient waiting. I leaned over and tapped Charlie on the shoulder. "Would you like this, Charlie?" It was a moment before he comprehended that this bowl of food could be all his. I poured it all into his pan. After a few wolfing gulps it was gone, then with an inquiring look he waited for more. I decided to serve breakfast for two.

Granola, milk powder, and a little butter lightly sprinkled with coconut would be my main course, followed by two cups of hot chocolate made with hot water instead of the lukewarm water I normally used in order to conserve fuel. Charlie would have six crackers liberally spread with butter followed by two peanut butter cups. For the first time on the expedition, I measured all ingredients. Time flew by as I carefully mixed and poured. Much to Charlie's delight and I'm sure amazement, I invited him to sit on the other half of my sleeping bag while I served our breakfast. A small piece of toilet paper made an excellent table napkin. Charlie didn't need one. He lay back taking full advantage of the sleeping bag. Background music for an intimate breakfast for two was supplied by the wind as it alternately whistled and roared around the shaking tent.

If time passed more quickly, the storm did not. The morning was almost gone but the wind was still thrashing the tent, its monotonous roar deadening my listening senses. I moved Charlie over and slid into my sleeping bag. With a grunt he ambled off to the vestibule and curled up for sleep.

I followed his lead and slept the rest of the day. That evening I prepared a meal of rice, butter, and instant potatoes followed by hot chocolate and walnuts. Charlie ate dog food with crackers for dessert. The wind roared on.

DAY 14

At about 8:00 A.M. the wind had died down and visibility had improved enough to allow me to leave. Charlie was in a playful mood and ready to go. He rolled on the ice scratching his back. I packed in a record half hour, happy to be on my way again. It was a relief to be doing something, something that would take me toward the pole.

I ran into trouble right away. The wind had packed the snow into rock-hard ridges from a few inches to two feet high with troughs of soft snow in between. It was very different from the smooth blanket of wind-packed snow that had covered the ice before the storm. Without skins, my skis slipped backward as I pulled my sled up and over the ridges. The skins would have given my skis the traction I needed. Now they were useless. I stopped and angrily released the bindings, disgusted at myself. It was so stupid not to have thought of this. With my skis strapped to my sled I started to walk, but found myself sinking halfway to my knees in the soft snow between the ridges. Dragging my sled behind me, I floundered through each trough, climbed over the ridges, then floundered again on the other side. Charlie was sinking, too, but his lighter body and sled weight helped him stay afloat. Thirty minutes later I decided to stop and replace the skins, but the wind had picked up, which would make the job difficult if not impossible. I struggled onward, trying to cover as much distance as possible before the wind forced me to stop.

I kept to a northerly course while angling slightly in toward the land to my left. The wind had swung back to the west. I was determined to travel at least a mile or two. Even with the wind and soft snow, it felt good to move again, but my progress was slow. After an hour of hard work I had covered only about a mile and the wind gusts were pushing me away to the right. My left side was plastered white with blowing snow. My face mask, while protecting my face from the icy blast, was layered

with an inch of ice. The left lens of my goggles had
fogged, then frozen, leaving me to squint from the right
lens only. Charlie's head was covered with snow, but
his body was partially protected as he walked at my
right side. He wasn't playing now. He was plodding
along, head down, serious.

In another hour the strengthening wind forced a halt.
All that effort and only two miles as a reward. I hoped
that in my determination to make at least some progress
I had left enough time to put the tent up. I anchored my
sled, tying Charlie on the sheltered side, then struggled
with my tent. I anchored one corner to the ice so that if
it got away from me I could retrieve it. Grabbing the
wildly flapping fabric, I anchored the poles along one
side and then the other. After much scrambling and
hanging on, I once more had a windproof home. I untied
Charlie, who made a beeline for the tent and was comfortably installed in the back half even before I began
unpacking my sleeping and cooking gear.

After a quick meal there was once again nothing to
do but wait for the wind to pass by. It was a typical
Arctic storm. The skies were clear, even sunny, but the
wind raced furiously across the ice pack blowing snow
into the air, blocking visibility. To keep warm I climbed
into my sleeping bag after moving Charlie to the vestibule. Sleep wouldn't come so I lay there listening to the
wind whistling and watching the tent walls shake.

At four o'clock the wind was down to no more than
a breeze. I dressed and began packing to leave. Charlie
was awake, reclining comfortably on my sleeping bag. I
kept him tied even in the tent, with his chain connected
to an ice screw placed in the doorway. My spirits were
high. I felt that the wind had at last spent itself and good
weather had returned.

I was packing the stove, talking to Charlie about the day's plan, when suddenly there was the sound of a single loud crunch at the doorway. We both immediately knew what it was. Charlie's head went up. He leaped to his feet and raced out the door to the end of his chain with a lionlike roaring snarl. Instantly I dropped the stove, grabbed the rifle, and scrambled out the door. A polar bear was twenty feet away staring at us. It had jumped back when confronted by a snarling Charlie. He was leaping at the end of his chain while I frantically fumbled for my flare gun. I finally jerked it out of my pocket and fired a row of flares at the bear's feet. It stepped hurriedly backward, then moved to my left, warily watching us. I kept firing flares with one hand and holding the rifle with the other.

I sensed something different about this bear. It would take a step forward and retreat only in the face of Charlie's vicious snarls and my flares. It looked thin and a thin bear could mean a hungry bear. My mouth was dry, I could hear my heart pounding in my ears, and my hands were shaking. My world, which had been so tranquil while I packed, was now shattered with fear. The sudden change was mind-wrenching.

The bear changed direction and walked back to the right, still twenty feet away. Although obviously impressed by our line of defense, this bear wasn't leaving. It was a standoff. I quickly checked my ammunition. I always kept two jacket pockets full of flare shells, the rifle was loaded, and I had more rifle shells at the ready in a row of loops especially sewn across the front of my jacket.

The bear swept to the left again, then surprised me by turning and without changing stride walked two hundred feet farther to the left to some scattered low chunks of ice. As I looked on in amazement two perfectly white cubs trotted side by side toward their mother. She led them to a wide slab of ice a few feet farther away, backed by a fifteen-foot-high jagged mound. Then she lay down with her belly to the sun and allowed the cubs to feed.

For a moment I wondered if I was seeing things and even forgot my shaking hands and pounding heart. It was a beautiful sight. The cubs were nestled close to their mother, feeding. Just a moment ago the bear had confronted Charlie and me, but now motherly duties had taken over. It was obvious that to her mind we were not especially important or dangerous. I was confused. I looked down and saw her footprint only six feet directly in front of the tent doorway. She had been that close and now, not two hundred feet away, she simply ignored us.

Nevertheless, I decided to strengthen my defenses. I zipped my jacket and put my hat and liner gloves on. My large mitts were too clumsy to use effectively with the flare gun and rifle. My boots were already on. I grabbed another three boxes of flares and laid them with a new box of rifle ammunition on top of my sled. I checked Charlie's collar and quick release. Everything was ready, but I was halfway convinced that the bear would feed her cubs and leave. I very much hoped so. I stood alongside Charlie, waiting. My heart pounded less and my hands stopped shaking. I had control of my fear. The next move was up to the bear.

After perhaps twenty minutes she got to her feet, nuzzled the two cubs, then walked a few hundred feet to the south. They followed behind right on her heels. Then, swinging in a wide roaming circle, she slowly worked her way through the broken and scattered chunks of ice, keeping her nose down, closely inspecting the area. Once in a while she raised her nose in the air as if trying to catch the scent of a seal. She appeared to be hunting for seals and had apparently decided to leave Charlie and me alone. She continued her close inspection of the ice until she arrived back at the slab where she had fed her cubs. She and the cubs milled about for a few short minutes; then, leaving the cubs among some low mounds off to the side, she turned in our direction once more. With the same familiar plodding walk she used while hunting with her cubs, she came in our direction and stopped a hundred feet away. Charlie, who had been watching her activity in silence, began to growl and strain at the end of his chain.

I was not only scared by her new approach but worried about her determination. She was obviously in a hunting mood, which I took to mean that she was hungry. Had she decided that I might be an easier meal than a seal? After failing to find a seal out there, she might have thought I was more available.

I quickly fired three more flares; then, holding my rifle at the ready with my left hand, I closed my right hand around the catch on Charlie's collar with my thumb ready to press the release. I felt Charlie's strong, thick neck muscles vibrating with his furious growling. The bear's eyes locked onto mine. She was a hundred feet away and every part of me concentrated, waiting for her next move, waiting for the first sign of her charge. Time stood still and the surrounding world had disappeared, leaving the two of us in a showdown for survival.

Then, ever so slowly, she stepped back a few paces and stopped. I didn't move. I kept staring into those tiny dark eyes, not daring even to blink. She raised her nose high as she swayed her head from side to side, trying to catch our scent. Then she moved silently to my right, flowing across the ice with unhurried strides, our eyes still locked. She moved back to the left, then circled around the back of the tent to the front again. I didn't dare take my hand off Charlie's release catch. I turned with her as she circled, keeping my eyes on hers. I slowly took my hand from Charlie's collar but remained at his side with the rifle at the ready. She continued to circle, not moving ahead or back. My nerves had passed the screaming stage. They were numb and my stomach was ice. Again I was faced with the same terrible dilemma. Should I shoot and get it over with or should I wait? I could only imagine the killing machine she would turn into if I wounded her. But waiting for her next move was almost more than my nerves could take.

Another looming question was what would happen to the cubs if I shot their mother. I knew the wildlife people would agree that I could defend myself, but what of the cubs? I was sure Charlie's snarling was a decisive factor in keeping the mother at bay and I was tempted to let him go. After all, he had remained unharmed after chasing bear number four. But I didn't want to risk Charlie unless it was absolutely necessary. So while the bear kept circling I would wait. If she showed any sign of changing tactics I would let him go after her. At least now I had a plan. As she circled the tent I turned with her, showing her that I wouldn't let my guard down, and I remained close by Charlie's side so that she would sense we were one unit.

The day had become years long. Surely she would give up soon. I was growing cold standing in one place, but I didn't dare reach into the tent for another jacket. My thinly clad hands were cold against the steel of the rifle. I could do nothing about it. My tactics seemed to be working. The bear was keeping her distance. But I was exhausted from the grinding need to concentrate. Finally, after what seemed a lifetime, she stopped and stared at me as if making one last decision. I waited, slowly lowering my hand to Charlie's collar. I was ready. Then she turned and walked in the direction of her cubs, stopping once to look back for a moment, before she went on to meet her cubs, who were scampering toward her. After a short reunion she led them away through their icy world in a northerly direction, head down, hunting as before.

I watched her leave and Charlie quieted down. We both knew we had won the right to survive. But it was only when she was out of sight that I dared relax. Overcome by nervous exhaustion I sank onto my sled, my knees refusing to hold me up. I began to shake all over and a wave of nausea swept over me. I vomited to the side of the sled, then looked up to see Charlie watching me. A look of understanding passed between us. Once again he had helped keep a polar bear away. Our bond of love was strengthened another notch.

It was time to gather my wits. The fright had eased, and my body wasn't pumping adrenaline in the same large quantities as before. I was cold, so I grabbed my down parka and slid into it. I looked north now and then just to be sure the bear and her family had really gone. I still felt a few twinges of anxiety. It seemed that time had been standing still, but when I checked my watch I found it was 8:10 in the evening. The bear had stalked me for four hours. No wonder I felt weak. I suddenly remembered the radio. The batteries were cold so I quickly lit the stove and held them over the blue flame to warm them in a hurry. By 8:30 I was talking to Terry and telling her briefly that we had been visited by a mother and her cubs. Her voice rose in pitch as she asked if we were OK. "We're both just fine," I replied. "No problem." I was glad she hadn't seen me a few minutes before.

Now I allowed myself the luxury of believing the bears really had left and wouldn't return. It was dinnertime and I wanted to do something special for Charlie. I cooked us each a bowl of rice mixed with a generous helping of butter followed by crackers and three peanut butter cups. I had lost several hours of good traveling time that day, but I decided to sleep for a while, then set out. The twenty-four hours of daylight meant that I could start anytime.

DAY 15

I awoke before midnight, looked out, and could see the low mound of Hyde Parker Island eight miles to the east. At last the wind had turned to the north. It was a beautiful clear morning and I decided to break camp even though it was midnight. I had had enough of stormy Arctic weather and didn't want to chance another delay. I was still mostly packed from my efforts before the visit from the bear and her cubs. Taking the tent down, I stuffed it in the back end of my sled and laid the radio on top. My sleeping bag lay along the full length of the sled with my batteries and cameras tucked inside. I never stuffed it into a sack. I saved a lot of time and energy by carrying it loose on top. I zipped the sled bag closed. Charlie was already attached to his sled. We were ready for an early start.

All around my campsite and ahead for a quarter mile there were low mounds of scattered ice, but I could see smooth ice ahead. I had put the skins back on my skis last night. I didn't really need them, but I couldn't afford to make the same mistake twice. Besides, I couldn't be sure what the ice would be like around the corner. I was only a mile from the top of Bathurst Island, where I would turn northwest. As I set out I looked at the view I hadn't seen in the storm. The one-hundred-foot-high cliffs to my left on Bathurst were ice-covered, with patches of brown rock showing through. Looking north between Bathurst on the left and Hyde Parker eight miles out to the right, I saw a wide blank area of ice, a dull, shadowless white in the midnight light. I hoped I wouldn't have to cross the gray patches of thin ice I had seen to the north as I stood high on the cliffs before the storm.

At first the ice looked white and thick. So far no problems. But as I followed the coast one mile to Cape Kitson, I noticed that the ice was becoming thin and slightly mushy, with gray patches where it was new. I stayed close to the coast as I rounded the cape, looking for an escape to the safety of the land. I found a wide gully that led to the top of a three-hundred-foot plateau. From there I could cut across the corner of the island and find safer ice on the northern coast.

Once on top of the plateau I looked across a breathtaking view. Long, rambling Loney Island was three miles north of me, separated from Bathurst by a body of ice-covered water called Water Sound, obviously in reference to the uncertain ice conditions. It was almost 3:00 A.M. and the sun was rising from its hiding place just below the horizon, pushing a wave of golden light across ice and land that was empty of anything human. There was total silence. The wind had left and nothing moved. It was an impersonal place, indifferent to whether I was there or not. It had existed for centuries and would continue to exist while I, a mere human, would soon be gone.

I turned away from my thoughts and walked northwest across the plateau, hoping to find an easy route down the cliffs of the as-yet-unseen north coast. The plateau was a tortured place, battered by winds that plastered the driven snow into rock-hard slabs. Patches of brown, sharp-edged rocks split into abrasive gravel poked through the snow and ice. If I could find no way around the rocks, they acted as brakes when my sled runners scraped across them.

Finally, I stood above the northern coastline. It was steep and icy, but a little farther west there was a sloping ramp that met the sea ice just before a frozen river mouth. Although steep, it looked to be the easiest way down. I unhitched Charlie from his sled, which he took as a signal to play. He bounded around in circles, daring me to chase him. Worried about our descent, I was not really in the mood for play, but how could I refuse? I ran after him, clumsy in my boots in contrast to his nimble twisting and turning. He always stayed just out of reach, tucking his tail in when I made a wild grab for it. After a few minutes I called a halt to the game so we could get back to the more serious business of safely descending the slopes ahead.

Tying Charlie's sled to mine, I turned them around and eased them down the slope, leaning back and using my body weight as a brake. The technique had worked well the other day and was working again. After a few anxious out-of-control slides, I finally managed to get Charlie and me, with both sleds, safely down to the coast.

Once on the sea ice I stopped to eat a handful of

walnuts, peanut butter cups, and crackers. Charlie shared in all except the walnuts. My raw, frostbitten hands were throbbing from time spent holding tightly to the sled ropes during our descent down the icy slope. They were beginning to improve very slightly but still bled and split easily. The blood froze my thin inner gloves to my skin, making it difficult to remove them without first thawing the blood.

The surface ahead was a mass of hard-packed snow swirls and ridges, some as high as two feet, a result of the wind funneled at high speed between Loney Island and the cliffs of Bathurst during the last storm. I elected to walk without skis because it was easier to move around the ridges, which were almost circular in places. After two miles I passed a long black gravel bar to my right, a part of Loney Island that reached almost across to Bathurst. Beyond, I saw a mile-long, one-hundred-foot-high finger of land stretching out from Bathurst to Loney, forming a wide harbor. Rather than going around the projection to save time and miles I chose to pull my sled up and over the gentle slopes. Ahead was Carey Harbor, a narrow, five-mile-long, almost land-locked area of ice that stretched inland on the northern coast of Bathurst. The harbor, as narrow as one mile, was hemmed in on each side by four-hundred-foot cliffs. And it was silent. There was no sound from the ice, none from the cliffs, and no sign or sound of wildlife anywhere.

As I stood looking ahead, loneliness again ate into my mind, reminding me of how isolated I really was. When I traveled through wide-open spaces, I didn't feel quite so lonely. But when high cliffs loomed over me, loneliness sat on my shoulders like a lead weight. So far I had traveled 107 miles, leaving the full length of Bathurst between me and human contact. The route to the pole would take me even farther away. I hurried over the packed, ridged snow, trying not to notice the cliffs, the silence, and the fact that Charlie and I were the only living things there. I didn't stop until I reached the far end of the harbor where the cliffs sloped away. I wanted to eat and feed Charlie before tackling a one-and-a-half-mile stretch of land that, according to my map, rose gently two hundred feet upward and then sloped down to a fjord through which I could escape the cliffs and Bathurst Island.

I climbed the slope, anxiously hoping that I would find the fjord on the other side. At the top of the slope, Saffron Hill rose to 585 feet on my right to the north. A rough, crumbly peak, it would be an unpleasant climb. Charlie and I kept walking until at last I looked down onto a long fjord that stretched north for two and a half miles. My spirits sank to my boots. Carey Harbor had been nothing compared with this. The fjord, only a hundred yards wide in places, was hemmed in on each side by five-hundred-foot cliffs, which rose almost straight up, throwing the fjord into a deep, silent shadow. The silence was overwhelming, and loneliness and the sense of extreme isolation again rushed over me. I dreaded going down into a place where I would be hemmed in, but it was the most logical route.

It was one in the afternoon. I had already covered twenty-two miles since starting out after midnight, in spite of the much slower pace of overland travel. I studied my map and decided to try for Allard Island thirteen miles away. I would go a long way toward making up time lost by the storm.

I walked down the long, white slope into the fjord, anxiety growing by leaps and bounds. Standing on the icy shoreline, I looked with dread down the shadowed ribbon of ice locked between high lifeless cliffs. It curved slightly, just enough so that I couldn't see the far outlet two and a half miles away. I put my skis on and set a course straight down the middle, wanting to put this fjord behind me as fast as possible.

All at once Charlie, who had been quietly walking at my side, pulled hard to the right. He had found polar bear tracks going in our direction. I stopped and looked all around, but could see no sign of a bear, and Charlie was only interested in the tracks, apparently not sensing a bear close by. I thought the bear must have traveled to the coast through the fjord just as we were doing. The tracks looked fresh, but perhaps the bear had passed through a few hours before and would be well ahead of us. I hoped so. Nevertheless I was concerned. If I met a bear here between these towering cliffs, I would be trapped. My sense of isolation increased as I continued down the fjord, but now I feared Charlie and I might not be the only living things in this shadowy void.

The ice was tinted green and almost snow-free. The skins on my skis kept them from slipping too much and I went as fast as possible. Walking beside me, Charlie slipped now and then but kept his balance. Once in a while I looked back over my shoulder to check for a bear, but mostly I kept my eyes ahead searching for the fjord outlet, willing my skis to go faster over the bare ice. In another hour I could see the outlet, beyond which was light, space, and escape. Finally, with a sense of relief, I skied out into Cracroft Sound. I was out of the fjord, away from the awful blackness and dread.

Without stopping I turned west, heading for Allard Island. I was surprised that so many places in such an isolated area were named, especially when no one lived or even visited there. Out in the sound the ice was snow-covered. There were no ridges or rough chunks, just wave after wave of hard wind-packed snow, crested like waves on the ocean. I was traveling northwest. A breeze was blowing from the north, and the sun, which was moving around to the west, threw its dazzling glare across the endless expanse of snow and ice but gave no heat.

We were approaching sprawling Ricards Island, which lay to our right, when I looked ahead to a mass that rose from the ice-covered sea in the shape of a perfect cone. I stopped to check my map. It was Allard Island, a four-hundred-foot-high mountain standing alone. The island had been a distinctive navigational landmark for the past few hours. As I put my map away Charlie lay resting. The day had been long and he was tired. I patted him, telling him that our camp was just ahead a few miles. He seemed unimpressed but rose slowly to his feet anyway, and we started out toward Allard Island.

With the cliffs behind us and wide-open space around me, I no longer felt the oppressive loneliness and isolation that had rushed over me in the fjord. My spirits perked up. I was pleased at the prospect of making thirty-five miles in one day. I was weary but seemed less tired than Charlie. Finally, much to Charlie's relief, we arrived at the tip of Allard Island at eight o'clock, just in time to make the scheduled radio call to base camp.

Taking my skis off, I climbed a six-foot slope and found a flat spot close by. It would be nice to camp on land for a change and not have to listen to the ice creaking with the rising and falling tides beneath my tent.

The sun dipped below the horizon and the temperature dropped to minus 21 degrees. I put the antenna up, placed the batteries I had been warming in my pocket for the last hour of skiing into the slots, and called base to report our location. Bezal was impressed at the progress we had made that day. I didn't tell him that the day had been twenty hours long.

SEVENTY-MILE

VOID

DAY 16

≡ At 4:00 A.M. I was jerked out of a sound sleep by Charlie's snarling outside the tent. I grabbed the rifle and flare gun and scrambled through the doorway. Shaking sleep from my mind, I looked around to see what was disturbing him. He was straining on his chain in the direction of the main cone of the island. I couldn't see any bears so I assumed one had walked by in the distance around to the other side of the island. Keeping watch, I looked for bear tracks around camp. There were several, but all must have been made before our arrival. In my haste to make camp last night, I hadn't noticed them. Charlie's snarling gradually lessened as the bear apparently moved on. I too relaxed. Although I had seen polar bear tracks all the way to Allard Island, sightings had decreased as I progressed along the northern coast of Bathurst. I would still have to keep my guard up. The threat of meeting a polar bear would continue all the way to the pole. This was their territory, not mine, and I could expect no relief from the fear of another encounter.

After such a sudden awakening, I saw no point in returning to my sleeping bag. The sun was up and the sky was a clear, pale blue with just a whisper of a breeze. I pulled my down parka on and took my map out to study the route from where I stood on Allard Island. When making my final plans at base camp to travel northwest from Allard to Sherard Osborn Island, then continuing northwest to King Christian Island, I knew the stretch from Osborn to King Christian would present the most challenging navigation of the whole journey. But this route would give me the advantage of traveling extensively within the magnetic pole area where I could record in detail everything I saw as part of the educational project that would go into classrooms in the United States and Canada. It would also satisfy my own curiosity and need to see and touch the islands surrounding the estimated position of the magnetic pole.

The challenge to my navigational skill would be two-fold. First, because the route would take me through a vast area of sea ice, I would have to navigate out of sight of land. And second, I could not use the most basic of navigational tools, the magnetic compass, which is rendered useless so close to the magnetic pole. As I looked at the route on my map, carefully considering all the complications, I thought through the various navigational methods I could use to arrive at King Christian Island. The night before, when I radioed base camp, Bezal had relayed a promising forecast from the weather station, which would be a decided advantage, and I decided to go for it. If I took the easier route farther west, I knew I would always regret having given up a unique opportunity. I folded the well-worn map and shoved it into my jacket pocket, excited by this new challenge.

I fed Charlie, ate breakfast, and packed my sled. I contemplated the possibility of again taking the skins off my skis. Without them I could comfortably keep up a two-mile-per-hour cadence. As far as I could see ahead, the ice was snow-covered, and now that my sled was lighter I wouldn't need the extra grip. I decided to gamble and took the skins off. By five o'clock we were headed northwest to Sherard Osborn, the last island before the route that would take us across a blank seventy-mile stretch of ice-covered, nameless sea. Sherard Osborn, for whom the island was named, had played an important part in the exploration of the northern Bathurst coast and the adjacent islands all the way north to King Christian Island, which he first sighted in 1853. However, it wasn't until 1916 that another explorer, Donald MacMillan, actually landed on the island.

After four miles of good ice covered with a thin sheet of windswept, packed snow, we reached an area of scattered ice hummocks two or three feet high. Charlie, who had been tired at the end of yesterday's thirty-five miles, had slept well and now leaned on my right leg as I skied, up to his old trick, in search of an automatic scratch. An Arctic fox appeared for a brief second, then darted away behind the ice to hide from us. Charlie tried to chase it. His sudden pull to the right on his chain caught me off guard and sent me flying. I landed hard on the ice and went sliding as Charlie, who apparently thought I was really getting into the spirit of the chase, kept pulling on his chain to get to the fox, which was now out of sight. When I yelled, "Stop, Charlie," he bounded over to me to begin a new game of bouncing on my chest while he shoved his wet nose in my face. Not to disappoint him, I grabbed him around his thick neck and wrestled him onto his back. Now ninety-three pounds of furry dog, skis, and I were well and truly tangled. I struggled to a sitting position, took my skis off, undid Charlie's chain, and stood up. He wanted more of the new game so I pushed him down again and scratched his tummy. We had by now grown so close that we could sense each other's moods and respond to them. My respect for Charlie was such that I did not want to appear fearful or foolish in his eyes. His good opinion was valuable to me.

The ice was getting rougher so I left the skis on the sled and walked through the narrow twisting paths between the uneven chunks of ice. We arrived at Ashington Point on the eastern tip of Sherard Osborn, where the ice was pushed into piles by fast-moving currents. Farther on the ice smoothed out, blending with the gently sloping coastline. I left the sea ice and walked along the icy shore for two miles to the edge of a narrow-mouthed frozen harbor, then crossed to Harvey Point on the far side, at the northern tip of the island. It was perhaps the most crucial point of the whole expedition. From here I would head northwest, leaving the islands behind me and navigating out of sight of land.

I looked at the blank, landless space stretching before me, totally devoid of any distinctive features. The ice glistened in the glare of the sun as my eyes sought something to focus on. But there was only bare ice in all directions until it met the horizon. I would be reduced to a microscopic speck, a tiny, almost unseen ant trying to find its way across that vast empty space.

I stopped and took out the map to begin plotting my course. I wore two watches, both set on Resolute time. I carried a twenty-four-hour sun-shadow dial, which I used in conjunction with my Local Apparent Noon chart. The LAN chart gave me the precise time the sun would be due south according to local time. A sun-shadow dial, while not considered reliable at lower latitudes, is an accurate tool in the area of the pole.

Once having established north and south with my sun-shadow dial, I laid my map flat and with my protractor I measured the exact angle west of north I would have to travel to reach western King Christian Island. My present position was 76 degrees 45 minutes north latitude and 99 degrees 35 minutes west longitude. From this position I had to travel at a thirty-degree angle west of north to reach my destination. Therefore, I would have to measure distance carefully to keep track of my latitude and longitude on the map. The measuring wheel attached to my sled would give me distance traveled, but as I skied up the coast of Bathurst Island, I had practiced a skiing speed of two miles per hour over smooth ice, which I had perfected at home so that I could determine distance, independent of a mechanical device that might break down. Allowing for movement of fifteen degrees each hour, the sun would be an excellent direction finder. The wind, which was by now a stiff breeze, was due north and would also help as a general guide, especially if it remained steady.

I also carried an experimental Global Positioning System unit, which was capable of giving me a satellite reading of my latitude and longitude. Because of the experimental nature of the unit, I had been advised by its developers to rely on my basic navigational tools and use the GPS unit only as a backup. With my position and course carefully plotted on the map and all my navigational information and tools in place, I was now ready to set out across the nameless sea stretching before me.

After an early lunch, Charlie and I headed northwest. The first two miles were through uneven shore ice and rough, broken hummocks. Then we broke out into smooth sea ice, which had escaped the torture of the swift currents. Later, to the east I could see an iceberg, perhaps thirty feet high and fifty feet long, trapped in the crushing power of the ice pack. Many ships in earlier Arctic exploratory expeditions had met the same fate by sailing into the spiderweb of pack ice to be crushed and broken. Abandoning ship, crews traveled overland in a desperate effort to reach safety, only to die of sickness and starvation.

Two hours after leaving Sherard Osborn, I looked back through the blinding white glare to see the outline of the 492-foot Osborn Peak in the center of the island. The wind had increased to ten miles per hour and was enough to form the familiar ice crystals on my eyelashes. My mask was freezing up, encased with a layer of ice. Snow pushed by the light wind was drifting lazily over the sea ice across my path. I hurried on, wanting to take advantage of the good weather system sitting over the area. By late afternoon the wind had increased to around fifteen miles per hour with the temperature holding steady at minus 17 degrees, which, with the increased wind speed, produced a wind chill of minus 50 degrees. Not as cold as the minus 80-to-100-degree wind chill I had struggled through during the first week of the expedition, but still cold enough to freeze flesh in a few minutes. Rather than stop at hourly intervals, I preferred to ski steadily, stopping only to feed Charlie a handful of his food and grab a quick drink and a few handfuls of nuts for myself when the need arose. The moment I stopped, a chill crept over my body, making me shiver even with my down parka on.

Pressing on, we arrived at 100 degrees west longitude. We had traveled twenty-two miles since morning. It was seven o'clock and the sun was dropping for the first time toward a horizon uninterrupted by land. With clear skies and the wind blowing steadily at fifteen miles per hour from the north, I decided to ski until midnight. Even after the sun went down, I could judge direction by the north wind. In the back of my mind I hoped to reach King Christian in two days, but I knew that a more realistic goal would be almost three.

After already experiencing two storms, I wasn't about to trust the weather. I wanted to travel as many hours as possible across the frozen sea and reach the other side before another storm descended upon us. I didn't relish the thought of trying to navigate through a storm out there in the middle of nowhere. The smooth blanket of ice covered in waves of wind-packed snow stretched as far ahead as I could see. On I went, forever trying to press on faster, with Charlie and his sled at my side. He was growing more accustomed to the long days but showed weariness toward evening and rested longer at every opportunity as the day wore on.

The eight o'clock radio call went by with another good weather forecast from Bezal. I gathered the radio gear together, loaded it back onto the sled, and off we went on the last leg for the day. Later the sun left us to take up its place below the horizon, and now we hurried on through a gray, cold light with only the wind to guide us. The oppressive flat light made the minus 21 degrees seem colder. My ice-covered mask blended with a layer of ice down my jacket front. I took my goggles off now that the glare had left and pulled my jacket hood close to protect my eyes from the cold wind. But soon my eyes were tearing so much they began to freeze, so the goggles went back on.

At last midnight came with thirty-five miles covered in a nineteen-hour day. Charlie thought that was long enough. As soon as I stopped he stepped to his left and lay squarely across my skis. It was his way of saying, "We are stopping for the day." He didn't need to tell me twice. It was a relief to shed my sled harness. I unfastened Charlie from his sled, and with that certain sign that I had read his message, he moved off my skis to curl up between the two sleds. This wasn't the first time he had lain across my skis signaling it was time to stop, but it was his most emphatic message yet. After erecting the tent I invited him into the vestibule to eat his dinner and settle down for a well-deserved sleep. After a quick dinner, I too was sound asleep in my sleeping bag.

DAY 17

≡ My internal alarm clock was working well. I awoke at four as I had planned the night before. I hadn't brought an alarm clock with me because I could usually rely on waking at a predetermined hour. I awoke on time but the lack of sleep was apparent as I groggily crawled out of my warm sleeping bag into the un-friendly cold of a new day. The weather, my biggest concern, was just like yesterday, clear, sunny, with a steady north wind.

Charlie wasn't at all happy at being awakened, so ignoring me he went back to sleep. I wished I could do the same, but I hoped one more hard day would take me within striking distance of King Christian Island and this was the weather I needed to do it. We were away again by five, facing the seemingly endless sheet of ice that stretched to an unbroken horizon. There was nothing to focus on even in the clear early morning light. Yesterday the land had fallen behind, taking with it the landmarks that had helped navigation. By midmorning we were in a wide area of low, jagged ice mounds scattered about in random fashion. The way through was easily defined and they didn't hinder us. We crossed a set of polar bear tracks many days old that meandered off to the east. The wind strengthened to fifteen miles per hour, streaming low across the ice and hiding my skis and boots in a shallow sea of blowing snow that swept across from right to left. Charlie appeared as if he were walking with no feet. Although reluctant to set out that morning, he was moving easily now, frequently holding his nose high to catch the smorgasbord of polar bear and seal scents that came with the wind.

It remained a sunny cloudless day. The wind although cold held to due north, helping navigation. I stopped each hour to sight the sun with my sun-shadow dial and, carefully aligning myself at a thirty-degree angle west of due north, I plotted my position on the map. To further establish my alignment with north, I stopped at the time close to noon when, according to my LAN chart, the sun would be due south. Navigation made the day a busy one as I frequently checked my course while trying to cover as many miles as possible.

As the hours wore on and the miles slipped behind

us, the wind-driven snow continued to stream across my path, making the ice look as if it were rushing sideways. I tried to focus on anything besides the streaming snow at my feet. The sameness in all directions was unbroken and I longed to see land once more. As the afternoon wore on the glare was merciless. I squinted, trying to see through the white curtain that hung all around me, but there was nothing to see and nothing to aim for in the distance. I hated to stop even to look in all directions for polar bears. At least while I was moving I was going somewhere, I had something to do, but when I stopped there was only the sound of the wind and I felt like an insignificant speck in an infinite universe. I started talking to Charlie, telling him of the things we would do together with Bill when we returned home. But out on the sea ice I couldn't relate to home and people, so I stopped talking to Charlie and concentrated on going faster.

Morning became afternoon, which had turned into early evening when we reached 101 degrees west longitude. Traveling hour after hour through the wind, which by six that night had increased to close to twenty miles per hour, was energy sapping. Its continual low moan, its buffeting, and the sound of my skis moving steadily north produced a sameness that numbed my mind. I forced myself to keep a brisk pace, knowing that was the only way I would reach land again. In case the increasing wind meant an incoming storm, I decided to continue until midnight as I had done the day before. Charlie was keeping up with the steady pace and hadn't protested yet.

Once again the sun began to set. That day it wasn't just a fiery ball, it was something friendly and alive that moved through the sky, helping me find my way across that blank empty place. As it sank lower in the sky I dreaded its leaving. I kept skiing, watching until its last orange glow faded below the horizon. When it was gone, it was as if a friend had left me out there all alone.

Finally, after a day that seemed to last forever, it was midnight and another thirty-four miles were behind us. After I put the tent up, Charlie walked past his usual place in the vestibule and spread out in the middle of the floor. He had claimed his spot for the night and wasn't moving. I planned to leave again at five in the morning so I unpacked as little as possible from my sled. When I threw my sleeping bag into the tent, Charlie immediately claimed the lower half. After pulling my boots off with fingers that were slowly healing, I pushed my feet under Charlie, trying to persuade him to get off so that I could slide inside the sleeping bag to find warmth. I wasn't making any headway until I held out a bribe of four crackers. Hesitating for a moment, he apparently decided the crackers were worth giving up his spot on the sleeping bag. After a meal of crackers, peanut butter cups, nuts, and two cups of high carbo-hydrate drink from my thermos, I disappeared into the depths of my sleeping bag, with Charlie curled up at my side.

DAY 18

The temptation to sleep beyond 4:00 A.M. was overwhelming, but when I remembered the possibility of reaching land this day, I forced myself to get up. Charlie was still asleep so I climbed out alone to check the weather. The wind had died down to a light breeze, a good reason to leave early and take advantage of the calmness. After two nights of only three hours' sleep I was in the sleep debit column, but the thought of seeing land spurred me on. Navigation had gone well and I was confident that today I would hit my target, King Christian Island.

My thermoses were empty so I lit the stove to melt ice and prepare a hot breakfast to make up for the skimpy meal of the night before. Charlie slept on and only awoke when I offered him a bowl of warm oatmeal. After breakfast I scooted around trying to leave by five and made it with five minutes to spare. Throughout the journey I had set goals for myself so that I always had something to aim for, giving myself a logical reason to hurry, to leave on time and walk and ski a certain number of miles each day.

We had gone only a few steps when Charlie decided to roll on the ice, scratching his back, after which he got to his feet, gave a mighty shake, and we were off once more. I took it to be his way of shaking sleep out of his head. His method didn't appeal to me. Instead I yawned my way through the process, taking the first half mile to really wake up. Even though I was sleepy, my spirits were buoyant. The wind was still from the north but only a breeze, a relief from the windy toil-worn hours of yesterday. I maintained a constant thirty-degree angle from north, having taken the day's first reading from the sun for direction and using the northerly wind as a ready reference.

Over to the west I could see the outline of another iceberg far away, trapped as the others had been. We passed through two hundred yards of low, wide mounds of multiyear ice, worn smooth and shaded with varied hues of blue. Ahead, I could faintly see a strip of ice twenty feet wide stretching east to west that wasn't quite the clear white of the older ice. Its grayish tint signaled new ice. There must have been a water lead that had refrozen within the last day or two. As I approached it, I cautiously prodded with my ski pole, testing the thickness of the ice. It felt solid so I hurried across. A few feet farther on I jumped in fright as the silence exploded in a deafening crack. By now I knew the sound of ice splitting under enormous internal pressure. A narrow split had pierced the ice in a long, jagged line stretching out of sight to the east. There had been many such splits over the last two days, a reminder that the ice that provided me a surface on which to travel was also a moving, changing substance over which I had no control. Charlie was unperturbed by these occasional loud reports. Perhaps he had heard them so many times throughout his life he accepted them as normal. Not so for me.

By midmorning the hazy glare was in full force. I had grown tired of straining to see beyond the white wall that reflected off everything, but I kept watching the northern horizon, searching for the land I knew had to be there. I had covered thirteen miles when, at noon, I thought I could see the faint outline of a low, spreading island to the north. I rubbed the ice crystals off my eyelashes, trying to see. It had to be King Christian. I skied on with a new energy born of the need to know if I was on course, if my careful navigation had paid off. Without stopping to eat or drink I skied faster, closing the gap beyond which I hoped to find the island I sought. After another mile I knew it was King Christian. I had intended my navigation to take me to the southwest corner of the island, but I saw that I was headed a little far to the west, perhaps a mile. After plotting the correction on the map I turned slightly north. As the island grew larger I reached 102 degrees west longitude. Taking time only to make a noon sun directional check, I headed with growing excitement to the island, now less than three miles away. It appeared in the distance as gently rising to a low center well inland. There were no cliffs or anything steep.

I was elated to find not only land, but the land I had been aiming for. I arrived at the western tip of what appeared on the map as a horseshoe-shaped bay at the southwest corner of the island. But it was impossible to determine its exact shape because the shoreline was so flat I could only guess if I was on land or sea ice. Looking around, I saw a desolate, flat, barren place where the land and sea ice met in a barely discernible line. Flat plates of two-foot-thick ice had ridden up in places over the land edge, pointing skyward at odd angles. The land was so low that it had been unable to stop the sea ice from invading its space. Rising only a few feet over a long distance inland, it had the appearance of a crumpled white blanket. I had to judge the shore edge by the difference in the ice. The sea ice was cracked and buckled. In contrast, the land ice was more stable, giving less under my weight and without the hollow sound of the sea ice.

The coast had no real distinguishing features other than its own empty flatness. But I had passed no other island like it, which made it distinctive in its own right. Now my job was to prove to myself that I had indeed arrived on King Christian Island or, heaven forbid, some other island. The sun was 23 degrees southwest, and as I faced west across the sea ice the land lay at my back, telling me I stood on the west coast of the island. I could see a long, flat coastline stretching to the northwest. With my ski pole and protractor I sketched out angles in the snow and found the coast to be at an angle of 50 degrees from due north, agreeing with the coastline angle shown on the map. The map also showed the coastline at the southwestern tip of the island to be flat, with the land rising to one hundred feet more than a mile inland. As a last check before I moved on, I turned on the GPS unit, which gave me a reading that agreed with the one I had plotted on my map. Everything added up to King Christian Island. My navigation had been a complete success.

My next plan was to travel north, the length of the west coast, identifying landmarks all the way. Then, after reaching the only identifiable coastal bluff that appeared on the map, I would turn south and travel back down the coast to the estimated pole position. By traveling the entire west coast, I would continue to positively identify the island, then use it as a reference to locate the mean position of the pole. I would add the island to my list of navigational tools to find the pole's mean position and later to find my way to the place I was to be picked up by an aircraft and returned to base camp.

Charlie and I ate an overdue lunch before moving on. He was hungry and gobbled up a large helping of dog food before turning to see what he could wring from me. But he was too late; I had already finished my lunch and sat basking in the knowledge that I had found King Christian Island and it wouldn't be many days before we were at the pole. I wasn't sure how far up the coast I wanted to go before making camp, but I was anxious to travel at least a few miles and find something a little more interesting to look at than the flat, desolate place we had arrived at.

Another two miles of uniformly flat, ice-covered land

found us opposite a rising plateau perhaps a mile long not far inland. I stopped to camp just short of a low coastal gravel bar. From there I couldn't tell if the bar was even attached to the land. We had traveled only twenty miles, far short of the thirty plus miles of the past few days. But the good weather was holding and an early camp would allow both Charlie and me to catch up on our sleep.

As I was threading poles into the tent sleeves, two or three strong gusts of wind kicked swirling snow into the air. Another strong gust hit and something shiny rattled past my feet. As I lunged for it, it picked up speed, instantly blowing out of reach. I recognized it as Charlie's pan, the only one he had. With renewed effort I raced after it and with my best running tackle I dove, expecting to capture it. But all I got was a faceful of snow while the pan tumbled on. Finally it disappeared in the blowing snow and I was forced to admit defeat. Gone was Charlie's water dish and also the dish I used when I mixed oatmeal or added warm water to his dog food. What was I going to use now? After a few moments of thought, I decided to share my bowl with him. Although not acceptable in civilization, out here it was a practical way to deal with the problem. Besides, I thought, regarding bacteria, no self-respecting little germ is going to live out here anyway. If it seemed that my life had now been stripped of all pretense, forcing me to deal with reality in a basic fashion to ensure survival, I knew Charlie wouldn't mind sharing my bowl.

As I returned to my camp chores, it suddenly struck me that the wind had swung toward the south and the temperature seemed a little higher, signaling a possible approaching storm. Voicing my thoughts to Charlie I said, "At least we made it to the island before all hell lets loose again." But just to be sure, I lashed everything down securely so nothing more would meet the same fate as Charlie's pan.

I cooked a double helping of rice and mashed potatoes. How I wished I had brought a few packets of peas or beans. I was longing for something green amid all the surrounding white. At that point anything would have done, food, a notebook, anything. In my journal that night I wrote, "Next expedition my diary cover will be green, along with at least one item of clothing, and I must bring some green freeze-dried food."

Base camp gave me a good weather forecast when I made my scheduled radio call, but I found it hard to believe when it was being noisily contradicted by the boisterous south wind, gusting at twenty-five to thirty miles an hour and shaking the tent. I turned in early. I hadn't seen bear tracks for the last twelve hours so I allowed Charlie to take cover in the tent vestibule out of the blowing snow. At least we could both catch up on our sleep.

BLACK STORM

DAY 19

≡ I awoke at 2:00 A.M. to the cheerful sound of almost no wind. "Thank goodness," I thought as I carefully shook the ice away from around the sleeping bag collar so that when I sat up it wouldn't slide down my neck. Every night my breath froze around the top of the sleeping bag as I slept, circling my head with an icy garland, which rapidly became my pet hate of the expedition. Then there was always the problem of ice forming on the tent roof and walls. In such a confined space every move brought at least a minor and sometimes a major snow shower, which always went down my neck.

That morning I was unusually successful in avoiding the usual snow shower and crawled out of the tent apprehensively to check the weather. The sky was clear, but the south wind was a persistent worry. After breakfast I hitched Charlie to his sled and, snapping the pull ropes of my sled to my waist harness, set off with the drifting south breeze at our backs. Now that I was traveling up the coast of King Christian Island, I felt that I was at last on the final leg of the expedition.

The island continued to look like the desolate, flat moonscape of the day before, its coastline barely discernible, its barren icy plains stretching far inland, gently rising to low hills. The silence wrung the life out of all it touched. In a short time we arrived at the dark brown patch I had seen ahead of our camp yesterday. It was a shallow gravel beach at the mouths of two ribbons of rivers that wound their way down from the inland hills over the coastal plains to the sea. A few hundred yards ahead another shallow river lay parallel to the first two, all three providing a summer drainage system off the inland hills. At first the coastal edge was straight, defined mostly by plates of ice pushed up onto the low shore and by the fragile, buckled ice that rose and fell with the tides. The ice was roughest around the first two river mouths, forcing me to ski close to shore, which made Charlie unhappy and hesitant about walking over the thin, cracked ice.

At two miles the coast swung out in a curving bite, then swept northwest to Sutherland Point, which, rather than a point, was a wide projection of flat land opening to a remarkable wide plain, so flat in places that it did not show a single wrinkle in its icy cover. A bay beyond revealed the effects of tidal currents sweeping around the point. Plates of ice pushed upward at steep

angles forced me to swing wide, much to Charlie's relief, to find flat ice. The ice creaked like an old ship, even
moving and buckling in front of us, and the noise made
Charlie jump backward. I didn't like it either. Any sound
in the silence was magnified, causing my nerves to react
to the slightest noise. It was not only unnerving but
downright spooky. I wondered if the tide was cresting
as we passed by, which would account for all the noise
and movement. I stopped to reassure Charlie, but he
kept walking, sending me the message that his reassurance would come when we left this coast behind.

The bay was over two miles wide and swept west to
a projection of land leading to the final stretch of western coastline. At the northern edge of the bay, I decided
to explore the Wallis River, which appeared to be the
largest river on the coast. In order to identify the river
properly, I would have to travel inland about three
miles. At first the river meandered its way through a
plain that rose and fell only slightly until I crossed the
shallow banks of a minor river coming from the south.
Later the main channel snaked its way through a
scooped-out canyon quite wide in places, and farther on
it occasionally brushed the sides of steeper slopes. Here
and there patches of gray-brown, sharp-edged gravel
showed through the wind-packed snow on the river
banks. Patches of orange lichen grew on the sides of
occasional scattered rocks. A few dried stalks of last
summer's grass remained. A 370-foot peak showed to
the north, although rather than a peak, it appeared from
where I stood as a high point on a plateau. The landscape, although mostly hidden under a layer of snow
and ice, had a sterile, wind-blasted look.

I had traveled up Wallis River far enough to positively
identify it, and it was now time to return to the coast.

But before leaving the inland spot, I went to my sled and from a small waterproof nylon sack I took four tiny mementos, one each for Bill, my parents, and myself, to bury inside a cairn. The gravel was sharp and frozen. A few blows from my ice axe loosened the top layer and with my shovel I piled gravel and small rocks into a two-foot-high mound far enough above the river bank to escape the summer thaw. I placed the mementos in a hollow I scooped out on top. There was a note from Bill that he had instructed me not to open until now. In his scrawling handwriting it read, "When you read this you'll have arrived at King Christian. Congratulations on becoming the first woman to solo the magnetic North Pole. We're proud of you. Come home safe. We all love you." I could barely see through my tears as memories of home rushed in. I placed the note alongside the other mementos in the hollow, then sealed the top with more gravel. As King Christian was to be the most northerly island I would visit, I wanted to leave something from all of us there, almost as if to claim a part of this tranquil place for ourselves. I had dreamed of seeing and walking on this island for a long time. Now I had, and a reminder of my presence would remain.

With one last look at the cairn I turned to leave for the coast and soon came to the edge of another shallow riverbed pointing silently toward the distant shore. I crossed to the other side and skied back to the coast, arriving at a place where the ice, only a few inches thick, had buckled and lay in broken, cracked plates several feet wide. Some had ridden over neighboring plates while others had been pushed to almost vertical angles. I stepped gingerly onto the first reasonably flat plate, carefully trusting my full weight to it. Charlie was not a happy fellow. He pulled back and did not want to cross.

I could see a route that looked safe and tugged on his chain until slowly and reluctantly he followed, balking at the cracks and gaps.

A few feet farther on my skis slipped sideways, dumping me on my side on a steep, sloping plate. Carefully regaining my feet I took my skis off so that my boots would grip the ice, but then I was more vulnerable to stepping through hidden snow-covered cracks. The ice moved and grated as it took our weight and I wished I had listened to Charlie's signals, but I was in the middle of it and might as well keep going forward. I was carefully picking my way around a particularly creaky area using my ski poles for balance when all at once my feet flew backward, dumping me again, but this time face-down. The ice had tilted with our combined weight and sleds, and I was sliding backward toward a gaping, water-filled crevasse. Frantically grabbing the top of the ice plate, the fingers of my left hand barely curling over the top for a desperate grip, I reached across with my right to help a wildly scrambling Charlie, who with his front claws was trying to stop his backward slide toward the crevasse. With a last-ditch shove from me and all his strength, he managed to get his claws over the top, pull himself and his sled up, and then jump to the next flat plate.

My plate by now was tilting at an ever-steepening angle with the weight of my sled dragging me down toward the water, threatening to pull my fingers free. Twisting my head as far as I could, I saw the back end of my sled already in the black water. If I had released the sled from my harness I would have lost all my supplies and equipment. Still, it was dragging me down and the thought of landing in the frigid black water sent new strength charging through my body. With my fingers clutching the edge of the ice plate, I performed a face-down chin-up, pulling my body and sled slowly up until, finally, my chin was level with my hands. I hooked my chin over the edge and, using my neck muscles as an anchor, threw one hand forward, then the other, so that both elbows were hooked over the edge. As I moved my weight higher on the tilted ice, hanging by my elbows, the top edge slowly dropped down to lie almost level, overlapping the next plate, where Charlie was standing. Scrambling on all fours, I dragged my sled behind me to safety and sat on the ice exhausted, catching my breath. Charlie leaned against me, licking my face, and I knew he understood that I had been in trouble.

As I sat there recovering I could see that the tilting plate of ice had been a seesaw balanced on the ice in front of it. Our weight on the plate had altered its balance, forcing the far edge up and its near edge down into the water. It had been a close call, and I couldn't wait to get away from this topsy-turvy area of unstable ice. The memory of the water-filled chasm practically snapping at my heels in anticipation of a victim was more than my mind wanted to dwell upon. And when I thought of what could have happened to Charlie I felt sick.

Shoving such depressing thoughts away, I stood and saw a route to the right that would work. Another fifty feet took us to safer ice, and when I looked back I could see that there might have been a sand bar separated from the coast hidden under the area we had tried to cross, perhaps causing the surrounding ice to be even more fragile. Without looking back again I went on, leaving the awful episode behind. One ski pole had cracked as I fell on the ice, but rather than stop to get the spare out of my sled, I pressed on, hoping the pole would last until camp that night.

Less than two miles away I could see where the coastal plain narrowed and sloped upward more steeply than before. I hurried on, excited to reach the coastal hills, which would be the northernmost point of my journey. The map showed a steep bluff, but instead I saw hills sloping up to two hundred feet, then sloping higher in places another one hundred feet to a plateau. I skied and saw where the hills curved around to the northeast to form the north coast, with another wide coastal plain at their foot stretching to the sea ice, probably with the same geography as the west coast. The hills on my right were a visual treat. Although of more modest stature than I expected, in comparison to the flat lifeless plains I had been exploring all day, they were indeed a welcome sight.

I had traveled only seventeen miles that day. My inland exploration of the Wallis River and the episode with the shoreline ice had made the miles seem longer. It was only four-thirty, but I chose to camp opposite the hills and prepare for careful navigation tomorrow. I still felt somewhat shaken by my close encounter with the seesaw ice and my wild scramble to safety. Charlie seemed to have weathered the incident well, but I was glad he couldn't tell me his thoughts. They might not have been complimentary to my judgment on this occasion. His good opinion of me continued to be important.

As I set up camp I wondered if Charlie had sensed that that particular sheet of ice would tip. He had been unusually reluctant to follow me, even jerking his head away when I pulled his chain. It was the first time he had expressed any disobedience. He was an intelligent fellow and the Arctic was his home. Perhaps I should have allowed him to use his own judgment. I stopped working on the tent to give him an extra hug. By now I knew there were many things Charlie could have taught me if he were able to speak. But if he was disappointed in my inability to understand his concern back there, there was nothing I could do about it now. I was glad he loved me anyway.

I had just finished putting up my tent when I heard the faint sound of an aircraft. It flew straight toward me at a low altitude. I waved my arms in excitement and the Twin Otter dipped its wings as it flew by. Turning sharply, it again flew slowly over me and I gave a double thumbs-up to signal that I was all right. The plane was so close I could see the pilot and passengers waving. They were engineers and scientists, I suspected, who were taking a brief flight into the frozen north to collect samples to help them in their study of the Arctic environment. Feeling not quite so alone, I watched the plane fly north until it disappeared.

To record the northernmost position on my journey, I decided to photograph Charlie and me in front of the tent with the hills of King Christian in the background. After setting up the camera on its tripod, I called to Charlie, who was lying inside the tent comfortably stretched out on my sleeping bag. There was no response. I reached in and tugged on his chain. Still no response. Obviously only something special would tempt him to leave such a comfortable bed. So I took the stove and saucepan out of the sled and with a great deal of noisy rattling I pretended to begin cooking. Charlie sat up and peeked outside the tent to see what was going on, but he retreated again when there was no food in sight. Only his favorite crackers and peanut butter cups would do the trick. I laid a handful of each just outside the doorway. "Come on, Charlie," I urged. "Come outside and have your photo taken."

The temptation of food temporarily overcame Charlie's desire to sleep, and after a long stretch, he walked out and began munching on the crackers. But by the time I had focused the camera, set the timer, and hurried over to stand beside him, he had finished all the crackers and peanut butter cups and was returning to the sleeping bag. Leading him outside the tent again, I pushed him into a sitting position, then ran to the camera and pressed the shutter twice before he got up and disappeared into the tent again. I hoped the two shots would be good enough because he had absolutely no interest in posing for another photo that night.

The base camp radio call brought the news that there was a storm system approaching. I hoped it was wrong. Although the wind still came from the south, it was only a breeze, and occasional high-altitude ice-filled clouds streaked the sky. If only the weather would cooperate at least until I reached the mean position of the pole. It was a mere thirty miles away to the south.

DAY 20

≡ I awoke at 12:30 A.M. and the first thing I saw when I checked the weather were the lenticular clouds, some cigar-shaped and others saucerlike, floating lazily across the pale blue sky. They and polar bears were the last things I wanted to see. I nervously checked the temperature. It had risen to plus 5 degrees and the south wind had strengthened to ten miles per hour. With sinking spirits I realized last night's weather forecast was correct after all. My quandary then was whether to try to beat the weather to the pole or stay where I was, close to the coast, and wait out the storm. I knew that at this time of the year storms can have long staying power. But there was always the possibility that the storm might dissipate before developing into anything serious.

I weighed the alternative. If I tried to race the storm to the pole and didn't make it, then I would have to camp out there and wait for it to pass. I had certainly camped in worse places and I had already weathered high winds. My tent and gear were in good shape and should be able to withstand a battering. Besides, could I really expect more shelter from the storm where I was camped than out on the sea ice further south? As soon as I asked myself the question I knew the answer was no. Therefore there was no advantage in waiting. I decided to go for it.

I hurriedly packed and with Charlie in his usual place at my right side, I set off at 1:00 A.M. for the pole. My plan was to head due south, straight down the coastline of King Christian Island, then continue to the south and reach the pole in one day. Navigation would be easy until I was out of sight of land again. Then I would switch to the methods I had used to get to King Christian Island on the way north. I skied down the coast into the head wind, taking a line farther out from the coast than I had on the way up, and again was struck by the flat moonscape of the island. It was almost as if the sea only reluctantly gave up the land and allowed it to rise gradually to form low hills. I passed the slash that was the Wallis River as quickly as my skis would take me, keeping my eye on the developing lenticular clouds. The wind was now steady from the southeast.

I reached the southern tip of King Christian and turned back for one last long look at the strangest, loneliest island I had ever seen. As a land mass it was an understatement, but I would always remember it. When I was planning for the journey, the island had taken on a romantic aura because it would be my northernmost point and important to my navigation. Now as I was about to leave it, it still was a romantic place, splendidly alone, silent, with no sign of life anywhere. I finally turned away to concentrate on the task of navigating across the same blank landless space I had traveled through on the way north. After taking careful directional checks of the sun and wind, I left King Christian Island behind and headed south. The pole was only nineteen miles away.

By four o'clock an enormous wall of blue-black clouds stretching miles across was building up and moving in from the south. The uninterrupted horizon allowed me to see an entire storm front in one overwhelming view. The wind gusted strongly at times, swirling snow high into the air. The sun disappeared behind the mass of clouds, but before it did, I checked its direction and that, combined with various directional checks all day, told me the wind was still southeast and I was steering a straight course due south. The wind continued to increase, but not enough to stop travel. The great ugly mass of black clouds in the distance appeared to be moving closer, but sideways to my path. It looked as if I would catch only the extreme edge of the storm as it went by.

Skiing at a two-mile-per-hour pace, I was closing in on the pole. But sometime after four o'clock, I saw to my horror that the boiling mass of thick clouds from the far distance was racing low across the ice behind a great wall of wind-driven snow straight at us. I stopped and, grabbing the bag of ice screws, I quickly anchored everything securely to the ice, starting with Charlie on his chain, then his sled, then my larger, higher sled anchored at both ends. It would be our only protection from the full blast of the wind. I shoved my arms into my down parka and stuffed my overmitts into the pockets. Then, with everything as ready and as secure as it could be, I hurriedly took the tent out. There was no time to put it up, but I knew I could wrap it around me as I sheltered with Charlie behind my sled.

Pulling the sled bag zipper closed, I was about to tighten a tie-down rope when I heard a sound like an approaching jet as the wind bore down on us with maniacal force. I raced toward the sheltered side of the sled, clutching the tent to my chest, but had only taken a stride or two when the wind plowed into my body, throwing me off my feet and down onto the ice with such a bone-jarring thud that my goggles were knocked off. As I slithered to a stop, still clutching the tent to my chest, my bare face and eyes were blasted and stung by particles of flying ice. Hardly able to see or breathe in the violence of the storm that seemed to suck the air out of my lungs, I looked across to Charlie, dreading that I might see him airborne. But I had anchored him well and he was crouched down, protected by my sled. I scrambled to my sled, half crawling in the hellish wind that was blowing gear away into the unknown. The loose tie-down rope had allowed the zipper to be blasted open and the wind was tearing at the contents of the sled bag, almost ripping it off the sled. Grabbing the zipper I yanked it shut, pulled the tie-down rope tight, then dove over the top of the sled to join Charlie on the other side.

Suddenly there was a pause. The first gust had passed by, but away in the distance I could hear more jetlike gusts coming. Then I noticed blood trickling down my face. Blinking my eyes to clear away the blood I felt my forehead and around my eyes. When my goggles were knocked off, the exposed upper half of my face had been cut by ice. I couldn't keep my right eye open. I was terrified that it was seriously hurt. I stood up to look for the first-aid kit, but immediately saw another blast of wind-driven snow and ice bearing down on us. I ducked just as it hit the sled and, in a sitting position, I pulled Charlie close to me and spread the tent tightly over and around us. A boiling mass of clouds hung over us as if trying to crush us into the ice. The sled took the full force of the blast, but the wind in its fury was not to be denied its victims as it reached over and around the sled, swirling snow and ice, pulling, tugging, and slamming at our bodies, trying to rip the tent away.

With my head on bent knees and blood trickling from my face and eye, I sat close to Charlie, hanging on to the tent. I could feel the wind slamming into the sled, jarring it into my back. The jetlike noise was deafening. I worried about the gear the wind might have carried away when the sled zipper had been torn open and I worried about my eye. I couldn't see out of it. It seemed impossible to survive the hole in hell I found myself in. A few tears mixed with blood trickled down my face. Then I suddenly realized what I was doing. I was allowing the storm to take over my life, allowing it to dictate the terms of my existence. "Damn it," I said aloud to Charlie, who couldn't possibly have heard over the din, "the Arctic has rammed everything down my throat from polar bears, to storms, to weird ice, and now this. I'll sit this storm out and beat it."

Charlie showed no sign of being impressed, but for me the whole situation changed from fateful submission to a fighting attack. I needed a plan of action. Without one my mind would only drift without positive direction. Just before I was forced to stop, I had checked my mileage at eleven miles for the last southerly leg. That meant I now sat only two miles from the pole. All I had to do after the storm was ski those two miles, then head for land and the prearranged aircraft pickup spot. I was almost there. Not even this fiendish storm was going to stop me now.

But first I had to stay warm. I couldn't stand up in the wind and inactivity was allowing the cold to sink its sharp teeth into my body. I zipped up my jacket as far as it would go. I put my overmitts on and slid the end of the tent fabric under me so that I wasn't sitting on bare ice. From an inside pocket I took the last two peanut butter cups of my day's supply, ate one, and gave Charlie the other. Then, smoothing one of the wrappers, I placed it over my right eye and tied a drawstring cord taken from the inside of my jacket around my head and over the wrapper to hold it in place, allowing my eye to remain closed more comfortably. Then, pulling the tent fabric closer around Charlie and me, I prepared to sit out the storm.

Charlie was curled up at my side. I couldn't believe he was sleeping in all that screaming chaos. The cold grew worse and I had to do something to keep hypothermia away. I worked to stay warm with isometric exercises, tensing one set of muscles for twenty seconds, then shifting to the next group. I moved fingers, toes, ankles, shoulders, arms, and legs as much as possible in the confines of my tiny, sheltered space. My face and eye stopped bleeding. The blood had frozen on my face. But now that I had a plan for survival, I felt in control in spite of my precarious position. Optimism flooded my mind, leaving no space for negative thoughts.

Time crawled by. After an hour I was still pinned down behind the sled by the howling gale. The cold marched onward throughout my body. My hands and feet were cold but not frozen, while the rest of my body was shivering trying to stay warm. I pressed close to Charlie, who remained curled with his nose hidden in his tail. I was hungry, which didn't help with the warmth problem. I did not dare try to stand up, much less look for food in my sled. Food would have to wait. Occasionally I peeked out from beneath the tent fabric and saw a still chaotic storm hurling ice and snow horizontally across my world, engulfing me and reducing visibility to a few feet. My joints were cramped and feeling stiff and sore. The cold was unbearable and began to lull my mind. I did mental arithmetic to stay alert, but nothing seemed to stop the slow progress of creeping cold. As the wind continued to scream its fury, my mental arithmetic trailed off and I had to forcefully bring myself back to it, trying to keep alert. But the cold came on and on, and I became more sluggish.

Finally, after another hour the wind slowed and the screaming howl quieted. When it dawned on me that the storm had paused at least for now, I tried to stand up, but I was so cold and stiff I could only get to my knees, then haul myself up slowly. Every joint protested. It was as if the cold had welded my joints together. There was still a strong wind but it wasn't blowing me over, and I sluggishly thought that if I could get my body moving I would put the tent up. But first of all I had to warm up. So I stuffed the tent safely into the sled, then I windmilled my arms while I walked in circles. It was a pathetic slow-motion effort, but I kept at it, feeling the warmth slowly inching back. It took some time but at last my body, although not really warm, was an immensely improved version of the cold, stiff bundle that had huddled desperately behind the sled.

Once more I took the tent out and began putting it up, at the same time noticing that the wind was gradually increasing. I tried to hurry, but my fingers were still slow and my body, which seemed burdened by an extraordinary weight, wouldn't listen to my mind urging it on. Snow picked up by the increasing wind billowed into the air. Afraid that I wouldn't get the tent up in time, my body at last kicked in, warming as I shook the great weight off and regained strength. Now pure raw desire to survive took over. I had already anchored one end of the tent, even before beginning to erect it, to prevent a possible untimely exit. Now I shoved poles into the tent sleeves, working furiously to beat the wind. One blast almost turned the tent inside out and I was afraid a pole would break, sending its sharp end through the thin nylon fabric and destroying my only protection in this hostile world.

Finally a combination of poles, ice screws, and tie-down ropes anchored the tent to the ice. I could hear far off the approach of another screaming torrent, and as I prayed that the tent would be strong enough to withstand the full fury of the next round of wind, I ran around adding as many tie-downs as there were places to attach them, then invented more until I had no more rope. I dragged my sled into the tent and propped it against one wall to help brace against the wind, then attached Charlie's sled to an ice screw just outside.

As the high-pitched scream of the wind drew closer, I ran to Charlie, rushing him into the back of the tent. After one last check that all was secure, I dove through the doorway and took out a belay rope that I carried in my sled for emergencies, tying one end around my waist and the other to Charlie's harness. Then as fast as I could I hooked the rope to an ice screw just outside the doorway so that if the tent was swept away Charlie and I wouldn't go tumbling across the ice after it. Zipping the door closed as much as the rope allowed, I leaned against the tent wall to brace for the blast I could hear coming.

It hit with a thunderous roar, throwing me forward and snapping the tent upright. With feet braced against the sled I leaned back again, stretching my arms along the walls to take the next mad blast. The tent walls vibrated and heaved as if they would burst. The storm had engulfed us again but each blast was repelled, as I fought with all my strength to brace the windward wall. It was too wild for Charlie to lie down, so he unwittingly fought the storm as he leaned calmly against the narrower back wall, his weight helping to anchor the floor. He was unruffled by the fury that raged about us.

After struggling against the wind for about an hour or so, I detected a slight pause now and then that grew more apparent until there were lulls in which I could catch my breath. Then finally there were only stray gusts that snapped at us as if reluctant to leave. The main force of the wind had passed, but the tent still flapped in the swirling snow. I looked out to see that the clouds were still heavy overhead, blocking the light, leaving only a solid grayness. My inspection of the tent showed the only damage to be a torn-out tie-down grommet. The low profile and modern design had won through. I put the antenna up to call base camp. There were worried inquiries about the weather. After giving a description of the storm and my location, I signed off, anxious to take inventory of my sled's contents.

It was with a certain amount of dread that I unzipped the sled bag. My worse fears were realized. All my food, except one small bag of walnuts in my day food bag tucked down in the front of the sled, had been blown away, along with most of the fuel, a pair of crampons, two fuel bottles, the spare stove, a few items of clothing, and assorted odds and ends. I went outside to check Charlie's sled. It was covered with drifted snow but still tied securely to the ice screw. It had flipped upside down, jarring a rope loose and allowing several sacks of food to be blown away.

It would take seven more days to reach the pole and then get to the pickup point at Helena Island. I figured Charlie had enough food left for half rations for eight days. It was one thing for me to go hungry and thirsty, but a food shortage for Charlie was a different matter. However, he was in better shape, with more weight on him than when we left base camp. I had fed him well and he had learned to drink more water, so I reasoned he would be all right on half rations and could go back to eating ice for the seven days. Inuit dogs are used to frequent periods of starvation and have learned over many generations to survive under conditions much harsher than the ones we faced now. I hated to ask Charlie to go to half rations, but I knew that he would endure it, just as he had endured so much else on this journey.

Having assured myself that Charlie would be safe, I turned to my remaining food supply. I counted out five handfuls of walnuts. Not enough. I divided them again and came up with seven handfuls. Perfect. There was enough fuel to melt ice for one pint of water per day, not much compared to the two quarts I had been used to, but it would have to do. The next question was could I survive with so little food and water in this cold, extremely dry climate? I knew that women, due to their physiological makeup, can live off their bodies quite well in times of starvation, so I reasoned that I would survive. I understood the realities of going from five thousand calories a day to one hundred calories, and from two quarts of water a day, which is minimal, to only one pint per day while working hard in a cold dry climate. I would be fighting hunger, thirst, and weakness, which would make it difficult to travel the remaining miles, but I knew it could be done. To help the fluid problem I could chew ice and snow. I was confident that I could finish my journey. I knew I might be in for some hard times, but they weren't enough to make me quit.

As I sat there planning, I wasn't despondent. This was the Arctic, after all, and I knew that among the many hazards I might face, there could be problems at any time that would change the entire logistical picture of the expedition. I would never have begun if I hadn't thought of these problems and if I hadn't the confidence that I could handle them. There was something else that spurred me on, something deep down that I would understand better later on when I was able to reflect upon my feelings at this moment. There was a core in me that wanted to jump out and face this new challenge, give it a good shake and win.

I took out the signal mirror and first-aid kit to inspect my face and eyes. My reflection showed numerous small cuts on the upper half of my face, above the area my face mask had covered. My right eyelid was cut and one corner of the eye was very tender. Both eyes were bloodshot, swollen, and bruised, but my left was not cut. I looked like a prizefighter who had gone too many rounds. "I'm glad I've got a few days to heal," I told Charlie, "I would hate anyone to see me like this." I then thought, "What a dumb remark." Vanity seemed out of place here. My eyesight was fuzzy in the right eye and less so in my left. I covered my right eye with an eye patch to keep it closed and hoped a good night's sleep would heal everything.

I unloaded my sleeping gear and threw it into the tent. I fed Charlie in the tent and let him sleep there. He had been all that I could have asked of him that day, calm and obedient. I was hungry, but I would have to wait until tomorrow to eat and drink. The temperature had climbed to plus 16 degrees, an incredible change and no doubt a large factor in the storm. The wind was calming down and it began to snow. "If there are any bears around out there," I told Charlie, "they'll have to wait until morning." He was curled up asleep alongside my sleeping bag and didn't hear me. It wasn't long before I, too, fell asleep, glad to have got through that hellish day in one piece.

DAY 21

≡ The first thing I noticed when I awoke at 6:00 A.M. was the peaceful quiet. It was still snowing lightly. My eyes were painful and bloodshot, and the surrounding tissue looked black and blue. My right eye was swollen shut, but I could see enough out of my left eye to read my watch, map, and thermometer when I held them close.

I took Charlie out to walk with me while I tried to

decide if there was any way we could leave. It was impossible. The temperature was still plus 16 degrees, the highest of the entire journey, but it was snowing and the poor visibility was made worse by my eye problem. I returned to the tent with a heavy heart. Somehow I had to get going. I simply didn't have enough food to wait. I melted enough ice for my day's ration of one pint and I drank half but left the handful of walnuts until later. There was nothing to do until conditions improved. So, hoping that sleep would help my eyes and take my mind off my hunger while conserving calories, I climbed into my sleeping bag to sleep the time away.

At ten the tent sat ghostlike in a gray, silent fog that had quietly settled over everything like a soft blanket. Charlie sat in the doorway looking around, then, apparently deciding he wasn't going anywhere, he returned to his spot in the tent beside me and went back to sleep. I had to agree with him. The prospects for travel didn't look good.

Shortly before noon the sun peeped through, then the fog rolled away on a light southerly breeze. We could leave after I made a directional check of the sun for north and south from the LAN chart and sun-shadow dial. In order to save my eyes, rather than look at the sun as I took a reading, I used a fine piece of wire I carried for the task. It threw a thin shadow that showed the exact directional line of the sun. Now that I had realigned myself with north and south and determined that the wind came from due south, I knew which direction to travel. I was only two miles away from the pole.

After eating my walnuts, which didn't satisfy the hunger that had begun the night before, I set off with Charlie at my side. I was wearing my spare pair of goggles. The lenses of the pair I had lost were darker, but I was thankful for my habit of carrying a spare pair on all expeditions. Without goggles uncovered eyes are burned by the sun and glare, causing snowblindness. That was the last thing I needed to add to my eye problem.

My eyes and hunger seemed unimportant as I eagerly anticipated our arrival at the pole. This was to be the day. I kept checking the counter on the sled distance measuring wheel. At last it read two miles and I knew we had reached our destination. I confirmed my position with a satellite reading from my GPS unit. Then I hugged Charlie and it was time to celebrate. I set the camera on its tripod and took several photos of us standing there at the pole with the United States flag and the Canadian flag, because the pole is in Canadian territory, and then the New Zealand flag for the country of my birth, flying from a ski pole in the wind. It was one of the happiest moments of my life. I had overcome all that the Arctic had thrown at me and reached my goal. The surrounding ice looked no different from any other, the wind and the isolation were the same, but I had fought hard to get there and winning the fight felt good. That I was the first woman to reach the pole on a solo expedition was unimportant to me. It was the learning experience and the struggle to overcome the challenges that made the journey so rewarding and the prize so precious.

After I was satisfied that I had enough photos, I carefully put the flags away to return home with and to take with me to my next goal. The American and New Zealand flags had already been on top of several mountains over twenty thousand feet high around the world. As a sentimental gesture I left at the pole four tiny family mementos from Bill, my parents, and myself, just as I had left others on King Christian Island.

But I could stay no longer. Lack of food and water and the realities of what lay ahead of me in the coming days before I could reach my pickup point were vividly clear in my mind. Realizing that lost time now could spell trouble later, I hurried to begin the next stage of my journey. Thirst had made itself felt already as the extreme dryness of the Arctic air pulled moisture from my body that I was now unable to replace. I decided to save the last mouthful of water until camp that night as a treat. A gnawing hunger was increasing but I could do nothing about it. My day's allotment of walnuts had been eaten, so I would have to wait until tomorrow to eat again.

I took my map out to check the route I had plotted to arrive at Helena Island, the place where I would meet a plane for my return flight to base camp. Using the same navigational techniques I had used going north from Sherard Osborn to King Christian, I would head southeast thirty-five miles straight toward the center of Helena, which is a large island with high coastal cliffs. I should be able to see the cliffs from several miles north. Then would be the time to make a correction and head to the eastern tip of the island. I had reached the magnetic pole's calculated mean position, and my return route would complete a long, roughly triangular path throughout the entire pole area.

I began my journey southeast with so little food and water that I knew the next seven days would be a race to beat hunger and dehydration. I tried to hurry, but my left eye was pleading to be allowed to close and rest, while my right eye was painful under its patch. A thought lurked in the back of my mind that if I made good time I could finish the journey in five days instead of seven. I tried to ignore my eyes and the gathering wind, which kicked snow into the air. Long streaky clouds were filling the sky but were thin enough to allow the sun to shine through. I dreaded another storm. Surely we had been pounded enough.

After traveling only three miles away from the pole I had to stop. The wind-driven snow and my eyes made visibility impossible. I couldn't see more than a few feet. But just as I turned to my sled to take out the tent, the thought flashed into my mind that I really hadn't tried hard enough. I couldn't bear to give up my brand-new plan of reaching Helena in only five days. So I resumed skiing, convinced that there was absolutely nothing in the world that would stop me until I had gone a few more miles. My determined dash ended almost immediately when my ailing eyes failed to warn me of a lump of ice, which I tripped over, landing on my face. For a moment I was angry. Then it struck me as very funny that my grand plan had lasted about five seconds, only to end up with me in a heap on the ice. I laughed and tried to explain to Charlie what was so funny. He just sat there waiting patiently for me to pick myself up.

I guessed the wind to be somewhere around twenty miles an hour and getting stronger, and my eyes had had enough for the day. I groped around, setting up camp more by feel than anything else. My eyes worried me. They should have improved instead of getting worse. I tried to look at them in the signal mirror but couldn't even see that close up. The real shock came when I realized I wouldn't be able to sight the rifle let alone fire the flare gun or the rifle with any accuracy. There was no way I could see a bear approaching. I knew I was in trouble but there was nothing I could do about it. My eyes needed rest and I would just have to trust that a bear wouldn't visit us. I fed Charlie and put him in the vestibule. He was now my only warning, and my only defense against a marauding bear.

Then came the moment I had been waiting for. It was time to drink my last mouthful of water. Mostly by feel, I carefully poured the last drops into the cup. But when I reached for the cup I carelessly knocked it over, sending the precious water onto the floor. I knelt there, not believing what I had done. "Well," I thought, "so much for that. Next time I'll be more careful." But I was so thirsty I decided to light the stove and melt enough ice for the morning plus one extra cupful. By now I was looking at everything through a fuzzy curtain. No matter how hard I tried I couldn't see past it. I carefully felt the tube leading from the stove and tried to push it into the fuel bottle attachment. But I couldn't see the hole, so with infinite care I felt the hole with my thumb and guided the tube into it. It felt secure and I turned the fuel knob, guessing when enough fuel had been released. Then I lit the stove and placed the saucepan of ice over the flame, making sure it was level. Charlie decided to sit up in the doorway just in case the stove lighting meant some people-food for him.

I was kneeling there waiting in wonderful anticipation of drinking a full cup of water when suddenly two-foot-high flames spread out in a line sideways from the stove. Snatching an extra pair of gloves that were thawing out alongside the stove, I scrambled to smash out the flames, terrified that the whole tent was going to burn. I threw the flaming stove past Charlie, through the open door out onto the ice. Then, grabbing the sleeping pad the stove had been sitting on, I quickly smothered the flames.

The emergency over, I sat there stunned. It had happened fast. But Charlie had been totally unruffled when the stove flew by his nose, acting as if it was an everyday occurrence. He was so calm he could have said, "Oh, well, there goes another stove flying out the door. No problem." I assessed the damage and discovered that my woollen gloves had large holes burned in them, but they had saved my hands from being burned. My habit of always leaving the door at least partly open in case of fire and to ensure adequate ventilation from stove fumes had paid off. Otherwise the tent would have gone up in flames.

Then I suddenly had a new thought. What if I had damaged the stove when I threw it out the door? With visions of no water at all for the rest of the expedition, I anxiously went out to retrieve it from where it had come to rest in a snowdrift. It seemed all right, but I couldn't see well enough to be sure. In any case I did not dare relight it until I could see better.

It was time to radio base camp and tell them of my arrival at the pole. First I had to put up the antenna. Considering my eyes, I was tempted for a moment to wait until the next night, but I was anxious to tell them my good news. I could only guess whether I had aligned the antenna properly with Resolute. I took the batteries from my pocket and carefully placed them in the radio. With a short prayer for the antenna, I turned the radio on. "Kiwi expedition calling eight-one-five Resolute," I said, hoping they could pick up my signal.

"Kiwi expedition, this is eight-one-five Resolute," Terry replied in a clear voice a second later. "How are you?"

"I'm great," I said. "I made it to the pole today. I'm camped five miles south of the pole and I'm going down to Helena tomorrow."

I could hear the excitement in Terry's voice as she

replied, "Congratulations, that's really great. Bill called and sent his love. He's been worried about the weather up your way. Are you okay?"

I decided not to tell Terry about the storm, my diminished food supply, and the problems with my eyes. I was on the last leg of my journey and I could see no point in worrying everyone now. "A storm passed through and blew us around a bit but we're okay now," I said, hoping I sounded convincing. "Please tell Bill I made it and I send my love."

"I'll do that," Terry said. "How are your supplies?" She was being her usual thorough self and asking all the right questions.

"I have about ten days of food and fuel. No problem," I said, again concealing the truth.

"Good," Terry said. "I'll talk to you tomorrow night."

I signed off with "Good night, Terry. Kiwi expedition clear."

I put the radio and batteries away, wearily climbed into my sleeping bag, and patted Charlie good night. But sleep wouldn't come. I lay there thinking how ironical it was that while this was the day of my greatest triumph, it was also a day of near tragedy and possible failure. The fire had been a close call. My eyes were painful and almost useless, but there was no time to wait for them to heal. I had to reach Helena Island and my pickup place as soon as possible.

I felt frustrated and worried. I had prepared for all the problems I could think of that might prevent me from reaching the pole. Once I did that, I had simply assumed that I would have no trouble completing my journey. It was as if a climber had made an arduous journey up a mountain without a thought about how to get back down. But I couldn't bear to think of failure now. I had to find a way to go on. I knew I could make do with my scanty food and water rations. And the only way to heal my eyes was to keep them closed. Sleep was the best prescription.

As I snuggled deeper into my sleeping bag I pushed the thought of failure aside. After all, I needed to see only well enough to know where to put my feet.

9.

STARVATION

DAY 22

When I awoke at 5:00 A.M. my eyes were improved and the fuzzy curtain had mostly lifted. The temperature was plus 10 degrees, but to my dismay we were surrounded by a thick fog. The above-zero temperatures and southerly wind were still playing havoc with the weather. Now I was really worried about my inability to travel as many miles as I had planned. But I had learned on this expedition that the Arctic has a way of dictating the time and pace of travel, and I would just have to wait until the fog at least thinned. In the meantime I would take the opportunity to continue resting my eyes.

At midmorning Charlie woke me when he decided to move all the way into the tent and use my legs as a pillow. The south wind had increased to a brisk breeze, rolling the blanket of fog aside. I fed Charlie, who was in a playful mood, lying on his back for his customary tummy scratch. Then, after a quick eye check, which showed less swelling, I examined the stove for damage and tried to figure out why it had gone up in flames so suddenly. I decided that because of my inability to see, I must not have attached the fuel line properly and the resulting leak had ignited it when I lit the stove. This time I could see and soon had a pan of ice melting. After pouring one pint into my thermos for the day's supply, I drank the leftover cupful, slowly savoring each mouthful. Then I took out my precious handful of walnuts and ate half of them, chewing them one at a time in order to prolong my meager meal.

I packed and before noon Charlie and I were traveling beneath a canopy of thin, broken clouds and patchy sunshine. I kept looking for signs of lower temperatures and northerly winds, but the weather pattern seemed grooved into its present state of above-zero temperatures and southerly winds. I still kept my right eye covered, but even with goggles on the bright light quickly caused my left eye to water and deteriorate. The wind rapidly picked up, enveloping us in snow. Fresh from the last storm, it hadn't yet been packed by the wind and was blowing around us in a swirling mass.

I was traveling slowly, trying to make my eyes work, forcing myself onward. I knew that if I was going to reach my destination my eyes and the weather would have to change fast. My mood was one of frustration and desperation. I skied slower and slower. Then, taking my skis off to prevent a fall over some unseen lump of ice, I walked, pushing myself ahead, knowing that each mile I covered was one mile closer to my destination. My eye was running and the swirling snow was blinding, but I kept on. When my eye became so bad that I could hardly see at all, rather than stop I laid my hand on Charlie's back. If we came to an obstacle, I knew he would go around it and I could follow at his side. He was now my seeing-eye dog and the wind was my direction finder.

After five hours we had covered only three miles, a record for slowness. But I thought with some satisfaction that three miles were better than no miles at all. We at least were going somewhere, which was better than sitting in the tent fretting that I wasn't making any progress. Charlie was a champion. He stayed at my side just as he had done for the last twenty-one days and went straight ahead with my hand on his back. When I stopped he stopped. After all those days together he knew the routine and kept on.

I deliberately kept my mind off polar bears. If we encountered one now, there was no point in thinking of the consequences. Charlie would no doubt react but I wouldn't see it until it was in my face. In my imagination I could see a bear right behind me, but I didn't need that kind of mind torture, so I tossed the gruesome picture out as I had done so many times during the expedition. It was a slow, clumsy journey, but we were making progress. I considered stopping, but the thought of getting closer to my destination urged me onward. Finally, after another two hours and less than a mile, I decided I had had enough for one day. I hugged Charlie and fed him before taking the tent out of the sled.

I began threading the tent poles through the narrow sleeves, but my eyesight was so bad I had to hold the

pole and sleeve two or three inches in front of my face.
After much groping and stumbling around, I finally got
the tent up. But it was tempting not to bother with the
nightly radio call. Trying to find an excuse, I thought,
"It will be the first one I've missed and won't really
matter," but common sense took over and I warmed
the batteries and set the antenna up. I had promised to
call in with my location at the end of each day if at all
possible. The radio calls were my only safety net. People
had to know exactly where I was so that if I needed
help they could get to me quickly. A missed call might
cause unnecessary worry to those who cared about me.
It might also be the first signal that I was in trouble and
needed help.

I made a brief call to home base. I gave my position
and registered a complaint about the wind and weather,
but I made no mention of my eyes. Then I invited Charlie into the tent. It was a comfort to have him close
while my sight was so bad. If anything went wrong
with the ice we were camped on or if a bear came by, I
wanted us to be together. I felt cut off from the world
because I couldn't see it, and I needed Charlie at my
side so that I wouldn't feel cut off from him too.

As always when he was invited into the tent, Charlie
took that to mean the invitation also included the use of
the sleeping bag. There was one thing he hadn't figured
out yet, and that was that I needed more than a two-
inch strip of sleeping bag to fit my body into. I had
discovered that when I slid my feet under him he didn't
like it and moved over. I tried the tactic again and it
worked, but when I squeezed into the bag I found myself sharing the pillow with him.

I felt guilty about the pillow. I had made it at home as
a special luxury for this journey. In mountaineering cir-

cles people are laughed at if they take along a pillow. I hadn't told anyone that I had a pillow. After all, no self-respecting Arctic explorer of days gone by would have used one. But I reasoned with myself that I would have enough deprivation throughout the journey without adding the lack of a pillow to the list. Besides, I thought, as I finished sewing it at home on the kitchen table, it's such a tiny pillow, only half the size of an ordinary one, and really won't count. Anyway, my mountaineering friends wouldn't be there to see it.

But now Charlie had discovered the pillow and his big black head lay on it, leaving me with only a corner. Furthermore, he had fallen asleep and I could hear a soft snore. I had the choice of moving him or being grateful for the corner he left for me. After a brief moment of thought I decided to be grateful for the corner. My day's ration of walnuts and water hadn't made a dent in my hunger and thirst, but it felt good to lie with my eyes closed, reassured by Charlie's soft snore.

DAY 23

≡ Charlie moved over sometime during the night and I quickly reclaimed my precious pillow and slept well. I awoke at 4:00 A.M. to yet another day of wind. My first thought was of a storm, but it was a typical windy Arctic day with bright sunshine and blowing snow. Although the sky was still streaked with clouds there were no storm-warning lenticulars.

My eyes were greatly improved. I could see reasonably well and most of the swelling had gone. It was a delight not to have to look at the world through a curtain of haze. I ate a few walnuts, leaving the rest of my allotted handful until later, and drank half my water. My raging thirst could no longer be ignored, which meant that I would have to begin eating snow and ice almost constantly as I traveled. As I fed Charlie his breakfast, I found myself looking at his dog food with added interest. A thought came scrambling from the back of my mind that dog food was better than no food at all. But as attractive as the idea was in my now weakening, hungry state I knew it wouldn't be right.

When I brought Charlie with me on this expedition, I hadn't asked him if he wanted to come all these miles through storms and the other dangers we had faced. Yet he stayed faithfully at my side, never questioning me as he gave me his unconditional loyalty and trust. He had even saved my life. He was now on half rations, which he didn't appear to mind. He was his usual energetic self, but for me to take a single piece of his food would be a betrayal of his trust. Even if it would help me reach a goal that was important to me, that goal was unknown to him. One reason I pulled my own sled was that I wanted to reach my goal with my own energy, not that of a dog team or machine. Charlie was a companion on this journey. His survival was just as important as mine. The temptation to eat his food left and I felt twinges of guilt that I had even considered it.

The wind had turned conveniently southeast so all I had to do was ski straight into it, stopping occasionally to rest and, at noon, to check the sun and wind direction. The wind was strong and I leaned into it, forcing my way through. A layer of fine snow shaped like long, pointed fingers blew along the surface of the ice straight at us, reaching for us before dashing past, always followed by more. Billowing clouds of snow whipped into the air, blasting my body and plastering me with a white layer that froze to my clothing. Charlie's face was snow-covered and his feet were hidden in the blowing surface snow. I longed for the silence of a quiet day but this noisy, boisterous wind was all that was being offered. At least now I didn't have to measure distance. All I had to do was head southeast into the wind toward the cliffs of Helena Island.

My thirst grew by leaps and bounds. I grabbed snow and stuffed it into my mouth, but it held little moisture, so I stopped to chop small chunks of ice and laid them on top of my sled to be picked up and chewed as I traveled. Craving water, I tried to push from my mind pictures of a clear, sparkling stream running in an endless supply. The ice burned the inside of my mouth, raising blood blisters, but I had to have fluid. I was tempted to stop and drink the last half of my water supply, but I knew that somehow I had to find the discipline to leave it for tonight and eat ice during the day. The strong wind made me work harder and breathe more heavily, causing me to lose even more moisture as I breathed. The desert-dry Arctic air couldn't replace the moisture I lost with each new breath. Still I pressed on, head down into the wind, attempting to keep a steady speed to cover as many miles as possible.

The long morning finally passed. I stopped to feed Charlie, ate three more walnuts, and chewed another chunk of ice that made my mouth ache with cold. Charlie helped himself to a choice chunk of ice from the top of my sled. He was no dummy. After all, why scratch and dig for it if you can just reach up and share from the nicely chopped pile of bite-sized pieces? I offered him a second piece, which he crunched loudly. My mouth was aching so badly from the coldness of the ice that I wondered how he did it. Hunger gnawed at me continuously. A few walnuts weren't sufficient for this type of hour-after-hour slogging work. But I had no choice but to make do.

I found it to be a decided advantage to accept what I had and feel grateful for it rather than wish I had more. Wishing only made me feel even more hungry and thirsty, whereas acceptance and gratitude for what I did have allowed me to deal with the problem and channel my energy into moving ahead at a good pace. After all, arriving at my destination would solve my hunger and thirst. If I called in now giving my exact location, a plane couldn't reach me in these windy conditions. Besides, I had no thought of quitting. I knew I could push through and make it. As long as Charlie was all right there was no reason even to consider quitting.

The wind kept up its furious pace, always blowing into our faces, even trying to push me backward when strong gusts caught my body. Hour after hour I plodded on, trying not to notice the ache in my stomach and the dryness of my mouth. By now I was urinating much less as my body became more dehydrated. I thought, with a smile to myself, at least that solves the problem of having to go to the bathroom in the cold.

The wind increased as the afternoon wore on. I was concerned that I would have difficulty putting up my tent if the wind became too strong, although I could sleep in my sled if I had to. It was important to put as many miles as possible behind me. I decided that as long as I could travel I would plod onward. My jacket front was plastered with a thick layer of snow, my mask was a frozen lump, and my goggles were frosted all around the edges. By midafternoon the wind was sending me staggering as strong gusts of raw power sought to overcome my puny body. When the wind caught my ski tips, blowing them to the side and pulling me off balance, I took them off and walked. Charlie and I, both with our heads down, leaning into the wind, pushed ourselves through the wall of blowing snow. I moved the clip on his chain to the back of my harness, allowing Charlie to walk behind me so that my body broke the full force of the wind. The afternoon had gone and the sun was sinking in the west, and still the wind blew in our faces, driving snow down my neck. I stopped before eight o'clock to call base camp, then resumed the steady plod southeast.

It had been impossible to make good mileage. Just before midnight and after almost twenty hours of fighting to get through the wind, I finally decided to stop. I had gained another twenty-one tough miles. The wind was over twenty-five miles per hour with gusts well over thirty. The risk of losing the tent in the wind was too great, so I sheltered behind the sled with Charlie while he ate his food and I ate the last of my day's walnuts and drank my last water. It was too windy to light the stove even behind the sled, so I made Charlie comfortable on the sheltered side, checked the tie-down anchors at each end of the sled, and climbed in. After some maneuvering I was able to stretch my five-foot-three-inch frame out and snuggle in with my sleeping bag pulled around me. Not exactly deluxe accommodations, but I was cozy out of the wind and I could take a few hours' break from the struggle to stand upright and move ahead. Even the wind, hunger, and thirst couldn't keep me awake and I drifted into a sound, dreamless sleep.

10.

JOURNEY'S
END

DAY 24

≡ I awoke at 2:00 A.M. to find the wind had been replaced by a light fog, but visibility wasn't zero so I elected to begin the new day. I climbed stiffly out of the sled, glad to leave my cocoon, but soon became disgusted when it began to snow, cutting visibility altogether. Quickly putting the tent up, I fed Charlie and lit the stove to melt ice for my precious supply of water. Then I readied everything for travel as soon as I could see. At least I had my yearned-for silence. But this wasn't quite what I had in mind. It snowed heavily, covering the tent and sleds with a soft white layer. The silence and isolation were total. Even the ice lay silent beneath my feet.

By three o'clock the snow began to ease as the wind came up and the temperature dropped into the minus zero column. Finally, I could see a hundred feet ahead and decided to leave. The weather continued unsettled and I had no guarantee that a storm wouldn't come from the south carried by the tenacious southeasterlies. Without the strong wind I could move faster. But my stomach was weaker than yesterday and my mouth was so dry it felt full of cotton. My thoughts were overcome by the need for water. Eating ice wasn't sufficient to stop the onslaught of dehydration. I reasoned that I should be at the pickup point in three more days. I surely could make it. I tried to put the thirst and hunger from my mind, but it was impossible to ignore the craving, especially for water.

I turned my thoughts to Helena Island. I should be able to see it today. I wanted to see it, feel it, and set foot on it. Reaching Helena would complete my goal of standing on Sherard Osborn, King Christian, and Helena, the islands surrounding the magnetic North Pole area in 1988. These island goals were just as important to the completion of my expedition as reaching the pole itself.

By ten o'clock the hellish wind had returned to torment me. The unceasing noise of the whistling, howling wind, the feel of the wind lashing my body and face without mercy, and a savage hunger and thirst combined to make me dig into a reservoir of strength, discipline, and sheer desire to continue. I dug so deep that I came up with reserves I never knew I had. But they were there and I used every bit of strength to push my weakening body on. I was desperate to make more miles. I simply had to finish the journey now. The end was so near.

It became increasingly difficult to keep warm. My caloric intake wasn't sufficient to create warmth within my body. Whenever I stopped I immediately began to shiver and then it took an hour of hard walking to warm up again. In such a wind it was better to continue steadily onward, stopping only to take another piece of chopped ice from the top of my sled and offer Charlie some. I knew the ice caused my body to become even colder, but I had to have fluid. I struggled on, head down, with Charlie following closely on my heels in his more sheltered spot. The sun shone through white streaks of clouds that sped across the sky and the wind roared over the ice from the far distance. Now and then I could hear a higher-pitched roar as a stronger gust ripped across the ice to slam into my undefended body. I was in a survival mode, and although nature's fury was being unleashed all around us, I knew I was winning. I knew I could make it.

I stopped to make my 8:00 P.M. radio call. Then, looking to the south with the wind still thrashing and the sun low in the cloud-streaked sky, I thought I saw a dark shape in the swirling snow. My heart leaped at the thought of a polar bear, but the color was too dark. A strong gust made me turn my face away from the full force of the wind. When I looked back again, the same dark shape lay there motionless. I was afraid, but what was I afraid of? I stood still, my mind racing as I tried to comprehend what I was looking at. I had learned my lessons well about Arctic depth perception and I expected almost anything.

Then I remembered. Of course, it was probably Seymour Island. Battling the wind with my mind set on reaching my destination, I had forgotten as I started out that morning that I would pass by Seymour on my way to Helena. It was eight miles from Helena and the map had shown the island to be only one and a half miles long with an altitude of about ninety feet. I couldn't tell how far away we were, but now that I knew what I was looking at I hurried onward.

I should have been able to see Helena's high cliffs even before I reached Seymour, but the blowing snow hid them. The dark shape ahead of me looked like a whale lying on the ice. I corrected my course about one and a half miles east and in another hour I was close enough to recognize it as an island. It appeared smaller than the map showed, probably because of the sea ice that was piled up along its shore, hiding all but its highest dark crust, which barely poked through a layer of windblown snow. The ice was rough for two or three hundred feet offshore, so I stopped some distance away on the smoother ice.

The day had been eighteen brutal hours long. My gain of only nineteen miles had been hard-won. The wind was too strong to put up the tent, so once again I made my home in the sled for a few hours' rest. After feeding Charlie at the sheltered side of the sled, I ate my last two remaining walnuts, climbed into the sled, and pulled the sleeping bag around me. The sled rocked as the gusts hit its side, but I cheated the wind inside the zipped-up sled bag.

DAY 25

I awoke at 5:00 A.M. to a welcome silence. I eagerly looked out of the tiny world of the sled bag but my heart dropped with a thud when I saw a fog so thick that not a single ray of sunshine could peek through. I angrily shouted as I climbed out of the sled, "When is this blasted junk going to stop?" Not surprisingly, no one answered and Charlie didn't even raise his head. I couldn't see past the end of the sled, so out came the tent again. All I could do was wait until I was able to see at least a hundred yards away. Seymour Island had disappeared behind the fog and, of course, I still couldn't see Helena.

At seven o'clock there was no wind and the fog began to thin, allowing the sun to filter through. I packed up quickly and headed in the direction of the eastern tip of Helena. My energy level was low and although I tried to hurry I could really only hurry slowly. Charlie was in his usual place at my side and stepped along briskly, wanting to go faster than I could go. He had become used to a good pace, especially when the wind wasn't blowing hard, and now he obviously noted the lack of wind and thought we were moving too slowly. For the first hundred yards he kept looking up at me as if waiting for me to take the hint and get going at a pace more to his liking. I patted his head and tried to explain that this was all I could manage.

I chewed ice constantly. Snow didn't taste as cold, but it contained so little water it was almost useless, so I had to keep chewing the colder ice. The blood blisters inside my mouth caused by the burning cold ice were secondary to my raging thirst. One pint of water a day was no match for the long hours of fighting the wind and the sheer exertion of the hard-won miles. My stomach was so empty that the cold of the ice caused severe cramping, making me double over in pain. So I held the ice in my mouth until it was melted before swallowing. This was my sixth day of low rations and a serious weakness was setting in. It would be important to pace myself, and to make frequent stops, to spread what energy I had left over the miles ahead. But we were getting there. I plodded along knowing I could make it.

Around noon the fog thinned, allowing shafts of golden sunlight to penetrate my white world. And ahead I could see the glorious sight of the high, steep cliffs of Helena Island bathed in sunlight. Now I knew nothing could stop me from finishing the entire route I had planned for the expedition. Mercifully, the wind stayed away as I veered farther east toward Cape Halkett on the eastern tip of the island. From there my plan was to travel east across a three-mile stretch of ice to the Hosken Islands, a group of three islands joined to Sherard Osborn, the island from which I had begun the long journey through the magnetic pole region. I wanted to set foot on one of the Hosken Islands, then return to Helena, so that my triangular route through the pole area would be complete.

I would have to find a smooth runway of ice off the Helena coast for the pickup plane to land safely. Now that I could see ahead, I noticed with concern that the ice was rough for a long way out from the northern shores of the island. At base camp I had been told that the ice on the northern side might be too rough and I might have to go all the way around Cape Halkett to the southeast coast to find ice suitable for landing an aircraft. I hoped not, because it would mean a few extra miles.

By two o'clock a patchy fog had floated in on the continuing southeast wind and the temperature was plus 11 degrees. The weather wasn't going to improve until the wind moved to the north and the temperature dropped. The streaky, wind-torn clouds changed to an umbrella of solid gray and it began snowing very lightly.

Tiny flakes floated gently on a zigzag path down to the ice. Helena Island disappeared behind the curtain of flakes and I skied slowly in the general direction of Cape Halkett.

The afternoon turned into evening and Charlie and I still toiled onward. After stopping for the radio call at eight, we kept on through the falling snow, which sometimes changed to fog. Helena hid from my view, allowing me only an occasional glimpse. After fourteen hours and a gain of twelve miles, I needed to rest. My meager energy stores were depleted. I felt nauseated and weak, and my thirst was a torment. With so little food and water to replenish myself, I would have to get some sleep, which, due to the long days, had also been in short supply.

I made camp and with Charlie fed and asleep at my side in the tent, I fell into a restless sleep. I awoke often craving water. Once I went outside to chop ice and crammed it into my mouth to kill the thirst that tormented me. Finally, I drank a quarter of a cup of the water I had melted for the next day. It helped, but I did not dare take more because I still had another day of travel ahead, and perhaps more if the weather worsened.

DAY 26

≡ I could see a few hundred yards ahead when I woke up at 4:30 A.M. So in spite of the snow and fog, Charlie and I continued eastward, hoping the visibility would clear and I could see the cape and Hosken Islands. By 6:00 A.M. the snow was gone, leaving the fog to play games with the visibility. I had no idea when I passed Cape Halkett. It was hidden somewhere over there to my right in the fog. At around eight I could see land through the now patchy fog, but I was puzzled. I was looking for the Hosken Islands' most distinctive feature, on one of the islands—five-hundred-foot twin peaks rising side by side. The two peaks would show me exactly where I was, but through the fog I could only see one peak. The fog was rolling in and out, making it impossible to see anything for long, but each time I snatched a short glimpse, all I could see was one peak. Then it began to snow, cutting off any view of the land.

I took my map out with a sinking heart. I knew that about six miles to the east on Sherard Osborn Island there was a solitary peak with almost the same elevation as the twin peaks of Hosken. I had seen the single peak as I left Sherard Osborn for King Christian Island many days ago. It now appeared that in the fog and snow I might have passed Hosken and was perhaps six miles east of where I wanted to be. It didn't compute with my navigation and I didn't quite believe it. I turned on my GPS unit and the satellite reading showed that I was opposite the twin peaks. But I had to stop. I couldn't travel farther until visibility cleared and I could confirm the satellite reading with a visual sighting of the two peaks.

I took the radio out and called base to tell them I might be closer to Osborn than Helena so they would know all the possibilities of my location in case of an emergency. I hated to tell them I might be off course after traveling for so long on a mistake-free path and able to report exactly where I was each evening. But it was for my safety that I put my pride in my pocket. If, indeed, I was too far east, I was still determined to go back to Hosken, then to Helena, and finish my journey the way I had planned.

I put the tent up but couldn't rest. An occasional snowflake drifted down to settle on the tent, but it was the heavy fog that blocked out the land I knew was nearby. But which land was it? I kept watch, anxiously waiting for the visibility to improve. Finally, at eleven o'clock the fog lifted and there they were, the twin peaks of Hosken Islands. I was right on target. My navigation and the GPS unit reading had been correct. I called in with the news. Now base camp and I knew exactly where I was.

I had been able to use the experimental GPS unit only at crucial times, such as my arrival at King Christian, the pole, and then opposite Hosken Islands. Due to short battery life and other limiting factors of the new unit, I couldn't use it more often. But even with the advent of new electronic navigational instruments, the old ways were still reliable. I had relied on basic navigation throughout the journey and it had brought me, even in poor visibility, to where I wanted to be. I couldn't conceal my excitement about having navigated all the way with no mistakes, especially after the last two hours of uncertainty. My excitement gave my thirsty, hungry body a new burst of energy. "We're almost home, Charlie," I said, giving him a long hug.

The fog melted away, leaving everything bathed in sunlight. I broke camp and headed toward the three Hosken Islands. In a short time I was standing on the shore of the northern island about four hundred yards across from the unnamed twin peaks, their steep, white-streaked brown sides begging to be climbed. I was tempted but knew in my heart that I had to reserve my waning energy to reach Helena. Reluctantly I turned my back on the two beautiful peaks to look for the nearest smooth ice close to Helena for a landing strip.

As I skied toward Helena, I realized I would have to

find a landing strip somewhere on the southeast coast of the island. The ice had been too rough along the entire portion of the northern coast. Now I could see that it was even rougher in the narrow channel between Hosken and Helena where the currents played havoc with the ice, turning it into boulder alley. I angled straight down the southeast coast and, after four miles, I found solid, smooth ice, perfect for a plane to land on. I chose a camping spot about two hundred yards off the coast opposite a deep, well-defined frozen river mouth that could easily be seen from the air. I called the charter service and base camp to give them a description of my location. Miraculously, I had completed my journey exactly as I had planned. I had traveled more miles within the pole area than any other expedition. And I had done it alone. I had known that such a journey was possible, but now that it was almost over, I could scarcely believe what I had accomplished.

Before I began the expedition, Bezal and Ruddi of Bradley Air Services and I had discussed all the possibilities of a flight back from the pole area. Helena had emerged as the logical choice because it completed the triangular route I would travel through the pole area and because of the possible tie-in with a tourist plane. As it turned out, Ruddi reported that a tourist plane was to fly from Resolute to the mine the next day, and while the tourists stayed there, the plane would fly north and pick me up. Later, the tourists told me they wanted to be the first people to greet me upon my return. The major expense of having a special charter flight was cut in half due to their generosity in sharing their plane. After the pickup arrangements were made, Ruddi asked me to call at nine o'clock the next morning to give him weather information. Weather permitting, the two pilots hoped to arrive at my location about one o'clock that afternoon.

As I put the tent up, it suddenly struck me that this would be my last camp. I grabbed Charlie happily and told him, "No more camps, thank you, Lord." We were actually going home. It felt unreal. I had only one more task to complete before leaving. I wanted to climb the cliffs of Helena and stand on the high plateau. It was 5:00 P.M., hunger and thirst had caught up with me, and I needed some rest. But I had looked forward for so long to climbing Helena that I decided to do it early in the morning. I would eat my entire day's supply of walnuts before leaving camp for the climb and drink the pint of water on the way up the cliffs. That, I felt, would finish my journey in grand style.

About two miles before making camp I had noticed two sets of polar bear tracks, the first in several days. It would be terrible to have to deal with a bear now that we were so close to going home. I hated to do it, but I staked Charlie outside the tent just in case a bear came visiting. He wasn't too thrilled at not being invited into the tent as he had been the last few nights, but he obediently did as I asked.

I melted ice for my thermos to be ready for the morning. I had a half cup of stove fuel left. It was tempting to use it all and melt more ice, but just in case the plane couldn't get in tomorrow because of changing weather, I wanted to have fuel to melt ice while I waited. It wasn't time to throw caution to the winds. I still had to plan for emergencies. I ate my last two walnuts for the day, then climbed into my sleeping bag, but after only two hours, my thirst woke me and I tossed and turned. I got up to check Charlie. As I approached, he stood up and stretched, no doubt wondering, "When do we get back to a normal routine?" We had been going to bed late and getting up early for so long now that poor Charlie probably thought, "Here we go again." Since he was up, I invited him into the tent, but this time I led him in behind me so that I got to the sleeping bag first.

DAY 27

At last, at 2:00 A.M. of the final day of my journey, the wind had changed direction and the weather had cleared. I ate the last handful of walnuts and drank half the water for breakfast. Charlie ate his full day's supply, which left him one extra day's food in case the plane didn't reach us.

I stuffed a few clothes, my thermos, camera, and odds and ends into a lightweight pack and put it on my back. With the flare gun in my pocket and rifle over one shoulder, I set off toward Helena Island. I planned to walk up the riverbed opposite our camp, climb the steep banks to a five-hundred-foot plateau that was almost a peak, then walk northeast to stand above Cape Halkett. I moved slowly, trying to spread my energy over the whole journey. At least going down would take less energy than climbing up. The handful of walnuts had done nothing to end my hunger. After seven hungry days I felt nauseated if I moved too fast. To make progress, I had to stop frequently and not hurry. The water hadn't relieved my dry mouth and throat, but if I moved slowly I could control my breathing and not lose too much moisture exhaling.

In my thirsty, weakened condition, the five-hundred-foot climb to the plateau felt like climbing a twenty-thousand-foot mountain. But it was worth every step. The islands all around me were splendid in the clear morning light. The windswept open sea ice I had traveled both north and south looked boundless and empty beneath the pale blue canopy. I walked another three or four miles across the barren rocky plateau to stand above Cape Halkett. Helena was as rugged and steep as King Christian was flat and gentle. Its high cliffs and plateaus were stripped naked by the wind, and rocks were strewn about covered with lichen that existed in defiance of the violence it endured. King Christian was covered with finer gravel, grayer in color. Here and there a dried stalk of native grass raised its head, a remnant of last summer. Helena's steep-sided rivers carved their way down the cliffs to the sea, whereas the rivers of King Christian resembled grooves in the wide plains as they gently made their way to the coastline that blended almost unnoticed with the sea.

The Hosken Islands' twin peaks, sculptured and symmetrical, stood across the narrow strait. I could see all the way to Sherard Osborn Island and its lone peak. I looked north once more to where I had journeyed and thought of my last twenty-seven days, the struggle to keep mind and body together while overcoming the harsh realities of the Arctic. The struggle to survive the mind-wrenching fear of sharing space with so many polar bears. As I stood daydreaming, reflecting on my experience, I gradually realized several reassuring things. I realized that I had had the inner strength to make it all the way to the pole. I realized I had coexisted in harmony with nature, which sometimes can be unforgiving. And I realized my respect for polar bears had grown. Even though they had filled me with a terrible fear, never allowing me to let my guard down, they were simply doing what they had to do to survive in this difficult place. I had done the same.

And, of course, there was Charlie. He stood at my

side, his coat ruffling in the cold wind. Our bond of love had grown and bloomed. He had warned me of polar bears and had even saved my life. I had much to be grateful to him for. I knew he didn't understand why we had gone on this journey, but he had never questioned my decisions. He taught me patience and trust. I felt proud to take him home with me and I looked forward to teaching him the ways of another world he knew nothing about.

With one last look north across the gleaming white ice that Charlie and I had spent so many days crossing, I turned to leave with a reluctance that surprised me. But glancing down at my tent, which looked very small a long way below us, I knew I had to return to the business at hand. I had to be back in time for the 9:00 A.M. radio call, pack the remaining gear, and get ready to greet the plane.

The journey downward took half the time and I was soon back in camp setting up the radio for the nine o'clock call. "Clear weather," I reported, "excellent visibility and increasing wind." Ruddi asked me to call again with weather information at ten o'clock. I packed everything except the radio, tent, stove, and fuel. I kept a watchful eye for I had noticed another set of polar bear tracks as we walked to the island earlier. They appeared to be only a few hours old. There must be bears close by and I couldn't let down my guard until Charlie and I were safely in the air. I called at ten and eleven, then each half hour after that. The wind was increasing and I began to worry that the plane wouldn't be able to land. Another storm was due within twenty-four hours. I had kept my stove and fuel out so that when I was sure the plane was coming and could land, I could use the last fuel to melt ice to ease my madden-

ing thirst. But because the wind was in such an uncoop-
erative mood, I didn't dare burn the fuel. I might need it
for another day.

Just before 1:00 P.M., the call sign of the aircraft came
over the radio. Delta, November, Delta. The plane was
on its way and approaching. Very soon a Twin Otter
aircraft on skis flew low along the coast and dipped its
wings. It circled wide and landed. As it taxied toward
me, I took my tent down for the final time and stuffed
it into the sled. The radio went on top. The pilot and
copilot jumped out and greeted us. Charlie remained
completely unperturbed as he was carefully loaded
aboard along with our sleds. After the pilot handed me
sandwiches and juice, we took off in a cloud of propel-
ler-blown snow. I drank the juice and hungrily started
on the sandwiches after giving one to Charlie. Each
swallow brought back energy I hadn't felt in seven days.
I realized as I gobbled the food and drink that I must be
eating the pilot's lunch. But in my starving, dehydrated
state, I chose not to ask. I wasn't about to add a guilty
conscience to my hunger and thirst.

As we flew back over the ice to the Polaris mine, I
looked down, straining to see any sign of my tracks or
even a campsite. There was none. The wind had swept
all away as if I had never been there. Perhaps it was
better that way. After all, I had been merely a visitor
passing through. But if no sign of my journey remained,
the awesome presence of the Arctic would never leave
my memory. And now Charlie and I, after 364 miles
and twenty-seven days, were going home.

EPILOGUE

⚌ Charlie and I returned to the Polaris mine and an enthusiastic welcome from the tourists who had so kindly sent their plane ahead for us. The Polaris staff, some of whom had listened to my nightly radio calls, were relieved to have us back safely. I later found out that most people in that area who had access to a radio had listened in each night, following my progress throughout the entire journey.

Charlie and I had separate accommodations. Along with my equipment he was put in the same building he had slept in before our journey. I couldn't really feel sorry for him. He was fussed over as a very special dog and fed a luxurious meal of caribou meat, which magically appeared in an endless supply. I left him eating happily from a bucket of meat with the reassurance that I could return later in the afternoon to visit him. Then, after being shown my room, I hurried to the dining room, which was always open during the day. My first job was to quench my lingering thirst. The juice on the plane had helped, but I still needed more liquid. I stood by the lemonade machine and drank until I could hold no more. Next, I ate my fill of sandwiches and pie and, at last, my energy was fully restored.

I called Bill. "Congratulations, you made it," he said with a catch in his voice. "I knew you could do it." He had already called Mother and Dad. "They're both relieved you're OK and coming home," he said. "I called them every week so they kept up with your progress. They don't expect you to call them until you get home."

Home. What a wonderful thought that was. I went to sleep that night in a real bed in a building with a real roof over my head, with no worries about the weather or polar bears. I got a sound night's sleep.

Next day Charlie and I said good-bye to our new friends at Polaris who had gone out of their way to extend hospitality and kindness both before and after the expedition, and we prepared to leave for the short fifty-seven-mile flight to Resolute Bay to begin our journey homeward. We were the first ones on the plane and quickly settled into the two front seats that had been reserved for us. After a few days at Resolute Bay staying with Terry and Bezal, Charlie and I flew to Vancouver, British Columbia, where Bill and I had left our second car in March when I flew to Resolute Bay. The car, a Honda Civic, had been barely large enough to hold all my gear in March and now I had to find room for Charlie. He was too large for the front seat so I cleared a space for him on one side of the luggage behind the driver's seat. If Charlie was puzzled by this new form of civilized transportation, he took it in his stride.

I knew I had to find a veterinarian so that Charlie could be vaccinated before crossing over the United States border on the way to our home east of Seattle in Washington State. A friend directed me to the local clinic and Charlie, as unperturbed as ever, was vaccinated. While I paid the bill, I tied him close to the front door where he proceeded to dig up all the beauty bark from the garden around him. As bark flew in all directions, I raced out to stop him, but was too late. I borrowed a broom from the clinic and swept all the bark I could find back onto the garden, while Charlie looked on oblivious to my embarrassment. After all, he was just doing what Inuit dogs do.

Soon after crossing the United States–Canadian border, we stopped at a roadside rest area and it was there that Charlie was introduced to his first tree. He promptly lifted his leg but was too close to the tree and fell over. With a few adjustments he finally got it right. Then he noticed a large clump of yellow dandelions that simply demanded his inspection. He shoved his nose into their center and immediately came up with an earth-shaking sneeze. It was his first experience with flowers and pollen. Grass was another novelty. He rolled and played on the freshly mowed lawn, then decided to dig it up. With front feet working like backhoes, he rapidly dug a sizable hole before I could stop him. I hauled him away to the car to continue our journey.

I drove to the Seattle airport to meet Bill, whose flying schedule prevented him from meeting us at Vancouver. We had arranged to meet at the baggage claim area so that Charlie could be there too. I could hardly wait to introduce Bill to Charlie. I finally found a parking place, then discovered that Bill's plane would be thirty minutes late. I went to the baggage area but I was too excited to sit. I paced up and down waiting. Several people stopped to admire Charlie. He was wearing a new black collar and matching leash I had bought on the way to the airport. I felt like a proud mother.

Bill arrived at last, and as we met in a giant embrace he said, "Now I'm sure you're safe. I've never been so worried in my life." Then he bent down to hug Charlie. "So this is Charlie," he said. "He's bigger than I imagined. We both owe you a lot, boy." He took Charlie's leash and the three of us walked to the car to start the journey for home.

Our home sits on almost six acres overlooking the Cascade Mountains with plenty of space for Charlie to run and dig more holes. But I was concerned about introducing him to the other members of our family. First, he met Tom, our large cat, who is just as black as Charlie. Charlie had never seen a cat before, but I need not have worried. Tom took his customary swipe at Charlie, then allowed him to get close enough to become friends, often even sharing the same sleeping spot.

When our three other dogs were introduced it was plain to see that they peacefully accepted Charlie as the boss. No one challenged him in any way. We found that he was a gentle lead dog who retained a dignified position of authority, laced with strict discipline, over his kennel mates.

The goats were another story. There were seven altogether and none of them trusted Charlie, who, at first, was only allowed to inspect them through the wire fence. Snowy, a large white goat, seemed particularly attractive to Charlie, and when I later let him into the goat field for a closer inspection, he wanted to play with them all, especially Snowy. Snowy took flight and Charlie chased him, grabbing his leg just as I had seen him grab a polar bear. Of course poor Snowy was terrified, bleating at the top of his considerable voice for instant help. In a few moments I had Charlie separated forever from the goats. Now he talks to Snowy and the others each day through the fence.

Charlie adjusted quickly to his new environment and his new family, joining Bill and me when we hiked or climbed in the mountains, running alongside when we went cross-country skiing or took our daily ten-mile run. I sometimes wondered if he remembered his harsh life as an Inuit dog. I wondered if he remembered our hazardous journey to the magnetic North Pole. Perhaps it didn't matter. The bonds of loyalty, friendship, and trust that were established between us in that journey remained unshakable.

It was good to be home again, spending evenings showing Bill my photos, reading my journal to him, and sharing the details of my journey. Charlie was always close by. Bill was proud of us both, and although I knew he had had many anxious moments while I was traveling to the pole, his confidence in my ability to survive such a journey had never wavered.

Soon after my return, Bill and I began to plan another expedition, a journey on foot to the geographic North Pole that, this time, we would make together. Charlie was often lying at our feet as we pored over maps of the polar region and checked our route. The journey would present us with new challenges, new goals. But for now Charlie appeared perfectly content to stay just where he was.

ACKNOWLEDGMENTS

My thanks go to Tony Manik of Resolute Bay, from whom I bought Charlie. Tony cared so much that he parted with one of his valued dogs.

My thanks also to Phil and Dee Morris for their long-time support and unfailing friendship, and to Michael and Charlotte Buschmohle, our friends who have helped in so many ways, to Bill Bates for urging me to complete the manuscript, and, of course, to Jerry Torgerson, who taught me how to use the computer on which I wrote the story. Thanks also to Bezal and Terry Jesudason, who supplied base camp facilities, and to Tony Keen and his staff at the Polaris mine, where I began my journey, for their hospitality and kindness. And my thanks to the Inuit people whose advice on the ways of the Arctic helped me gain the knowledge I needed to complete the journey.

I am very grateful to Frederic Hills and Burton Beals for their careful editing of the book.

A special thanks to Sir Edmund Hillary, whose outdoor lifestyle inspired me as a young girl to follow the path through life that eventually took me to the magnetic North Pole.